The Lord's Church

ANDREW D. ERWIN

Charleston, AR
COBB PUBLISHING
2020

© 2020 by Andrew D. Erwin

The Lord's Church is copyright © Andrew D. Erwin, 2020. All rights reserved. This book, either in part or the whole, is not to be duplicated, transmitted, stored, or made available in any form without the written consent of the author.

ISBN: 978-1-947622-54-8

Published by:

Cobb Publishing
704 E. Main St.
Charleston, AR 72933

(479) 747-8372
www.CobbPublishing.com
CobbPublishing@gmail.com

Preface

A few years ago, I published a series of lectures I had given in classes at the Middle Tennessee School of Preaching and Biblical Studies titled, *Lectures on the New Testament Church*. This present volume is a revision and expansion of that work.

Some sermons have changed, some were removed, and some were added. My prayer is that the present volume is an improvement upon the previous effort and that the work will in some small way help the reader come to a better understanding of this vital subject.

The basics of New Testament Christianity need to be thoroughly engrained in New Testament Christians. We simply cannot overlook the importance of understanding the truth concerning the Lord's church. Let us be grounded in this truth, defend it, and teach it to all.

Dedication

Guy Hester was born February 15, 1936, in Vernon, Alabama. He preached 64 years. His father was S.F. Hester, a great gospel preacher. His brothers — Giles, Benny Wayne, and Johnny — each preached the gospel. Johnny is the last of these preaching brothers.

Guy's beloved was Shirley. They were married for almost 61 years. Wherever Guy went, Shirley was faithfully by his side. Whatever "stray preacher" Guy would adopt, Shirley did too. Both Guy and Shirley knew the importance of preaching the gospel and trained their children to realize it as well. To their union, four children were given. Ferrell and Tim are gospel preachers. Connie and Jalema are married to gospel preachers — Larry Montgomery and Jay Tidwell. His grandson, Guyton Montgomery, is also a gospel preacher and is the director of the Northwest Florida School of Biblical Studies.

Guy preached in Alabama, Arkansas, Indiana, Mississippi, and Tennessee. He even spent the coldest winter of his life preaching in Iowa before he moved back to a warmer climate. Guy did foreign and domestic mission work and helped to found and direct the Vreed-en-Hoop School of the Bible in Guyana, South America.

He preached for the Garfield Heights church of Christ in Indianapolis, IN, and the Southaven church of Christ in Southaven,

MS, as well as congregations in Ripley, TN, Ripley, MS, and Parsons, TN. While in Ripley, MS, Guy taught a "preacher training" class which helped to produce several gospel preachers, deacons, and elders. When moving from this place, he could not help his family pack for the number of visitors requesting that Guy baptize them before he moved. That day, on six different occasions, people came to his house requesting that he baptize them!

The two men who influenced Guy most as a gospel preacher were his father and Gus Nichols. Brother S.F. Hester and Gus Nichols were dear friends. Brother Nichols helped to teach and train brother Hester. As a result, Guy became acquainted with the Nichols family at a young age. Guy was also taught by brother Nichols in his Friday night training classes. These classes helped to train hundreds of men over the course of forty years. Back in those days, chart sermons were preached very effectively. The charts used by S.F. Hester and Gus Nichols would also be used by their sons. In fact, the first time I heard Guy preach, he used one of these chart sermons. He was conducting a gospel meeting for the Williams Chapel congregation west of Murray, KY, and the sermon he preached was titled "The Five States of Man." I continue to preach this sermon today.

The experience of hearing Guy preach led to a great friendship. He was more like a father than a friend to me. When my father passed away, Guy was there to comfort me and helped to conduct his funeral. Guy could hardly speak for the tears he cried. Guy was a veteran of the Korean War, and my father was a veteran of the Vietnam War. Late in my father's life, he began to struggle with his personal memories of that war; Guy would call him, listen to him, and comfort him as one old soldier to another and, more importantly, as one brother in Christ to another.

Many times, I would call Guy to ask him questions or to seek advice. Sometimes I would call him to bounce a sermon idea off him. He would usually say, "Not only do I like it, I want it!" That was just the way Guy was. That is one example of how he encouraged young men to preach the word.

When I think about Guy Hester, I must also consider the kind providence of God. I believe God brings such significant people, as Guy was to me, into our lives for special reasons. God knows our needs better than we can even imagine. God knew that this young preacher needed a man like Guy Hester in his life. He knew that Guy was the kind of man who would take a young preacher under his wing, encourage him, and love him. I am thankful to God for the men like Guy Hester that the Lord has brought into my life. Guy is not the only such man, but he is indeed missed, and only a void remains where once he stood.

When Guy would close a gospel meeting, he would use Paul's words to the elders of Ephesus. These words seem fitting as I reflect upon Guy's departure.

"And now, brethren, I commend you to God, and to the word of his grace, which is able to build you up, and to give you an inheritance among all them which are sanctified" (Acts 20:32).

Andy Erwin

Table of Contents

The Lord's Church 9
What the Church Is Not 13
The Church in the Mystery of the Ages 21
The Establishment of the Church 31
The Kingdom and the Church (1) 37
The Kingdom and the Church (2) 43
The Rule of Faith and Practice for the Church 49
The Church in Infancy and Maturity 53
The Structure of the Church Universal 57
The Structure of the Local Church 65
The Worship of the Church 73
The Work of the Church 77
The Falling Away 83
The Sin of Denominationalism 95
Is One Church as Good as Another? 101
Why I Am a Member of the Church of Christ 107
The Restoration Plea 111
Bibliography 117

The Lord's Church

Introduction

I.   As a matter of priority, Bible students should always determine to define key terms relative to understanding their study of the Scriptures.

II.   In Matthew 16:18, the word *church* is used for the first time in the New Testament.

    A. In this lesson, emphasis will be given to defining the word *church*.

    B. What is the church? What is the meaning and significance of the church? Is the church an essential subject?

III.   From the text of Matthew 16:13-19, we learn at least three important facts:

    A. Christ is the builder of the church — "I will build."

    B. The church belongs to Christ — "My church."

    C. The gates of hades/death (cf. Ps. 9:13) will not prevail against His church.

        1.) Christ's death did not prevail against the building of the church. His church was established upon His death, burial, and resurrection.

        2.) Neither will the gates of death prevail against the heavenly kingdom in eternity (Matt. 25:34).

3.) The last enemy to be destroyed is death (1 Cor. 15:26). Death will be destroyed by the resurrection of the dead, and he who has power over death will be vanquished (Heb. 2:14; Matt. 25:41; Rev. 20:10).

4.) The church is built by Christ, belongs to Christ, and will be victorious in Christ (1 Cor. 15:54-57; 1 John 5:4).

Discussion

I. The church of Christ is the *ekklesia* — "the called out" of Christ.[1]

    A. The church has been called out of the darkness of sin and ignorance to God's will to form the spiritual body and kingdom of Christ (1 Pet. 2:5, 9-10; Col. 1:13; 1 Thess. 2:11-12).

    B. The gospel expresses the calling to which we should respond obediently (2 Thess. 2:14).

    C. The "voice" of Christ is heard in the gospel (John 10:27; John 8:31-32).

    D. The church consists of souls who have heard and obeyed the gospel. They have been called out by the preaching of the gospel and have been added to the assembly of the saved upon obedience to the gospel.

II. The church is the "assembly" of Christ (Heb. 12:23).

---

[1] *Ekklesia* is a compound word from *klesis* "to call" and *ek* "out of."

A. *Ekklesia* is translated "assembly" in Acts 19:32, 39, and 41.[2]

B. Christians are not called out of our homes and assembled into a theater or town hall, but we are called out of the kingdom of darkness and assembled into the kingdom of Christ.

III. The church is the assembly that belongs to the Lord.

A. *Kuriakos* – "belonging to the Lord" – is the Greek word from which our English word "church" is derived.

B. *Kuriake oikia* means "belonging to the house of the Lord."

1.) The church is the house of the Lord (1Tim. 3:15; Heb. 3:1-6).

2.) The church is the "household of faith" (Gal. 6:10).

3.) To belong to the house of the Lord is to belong to the church of the Lord (see Acts 20:28 in the ASV).

4.) The church is the temple of God (1 Cor. 3:16-17; Eph. 2:19-20).

C. Two predominate uses of the word *church* include:

1.) A universal application to the church at large (e.g. Matt. 16:18).

2.) A local application to a congregation (e.g. Gal. 1:2; Rev. 2-3).

---

[2] Some debate has occurred over which definition should be used primarily for the church — the called out or the assembly. This is a moot point as every assembly is called or convened. Otherwise, there would not be an assembly.

        3.) Each context must be studied to discern which application is being used for *church*.[3]

  D. An interesting definition for *church* is found by combining the first and last verses of Ephesians.

        1.) Eph. 1:1 – "Paul, an apostle of Jesus Christ by the will of God, To the saints who are in Ephesus, and faithful in Christ Jesus…"

        2.) Eph. 6:24 – "Grace be with all those who love our Lord Jesus Christ in sincerity. Amen."

        3.) Therefore, the church is the faithful *in* Christ Jesus who *love* our Lord Jesus Christ in sincerity.

Conclusion

I.   The church is the assembly of all those who have been called out of the darkness of sin by obeying the gospel and being added by God to the spiritual body of Christ (Acts 2:42, 47).

II.   Anyone can be added to this sacred assembly and spiritual kingdom by hearing the gospel preached (Rom. 10:17); believing the facts concerning Christ as revealed in the gospel (John 8:24); repenting of sin (2 Pet. 3:9); confessing faith in Christ (Rom. 10:9-10); and being baptized into Christ to wash away sins (Acts 22:16).

---

[3] The various churches in the New Testament do not refer to various types of churches or denominations, but to various locations of individual congregations.

What the Church Is Not

Introduction

I. In our previous lesson we discussed some necessary ideas essential to providing the biblical definition for the church.

II. Equally important to our understanding of the biblical nature of the church is to eliminate some of the prevailing misunderstandings which have been provided through the teachings of men and handed down for generations.

Discussion

I. The church is not a denomination.

    A. No denominations are found in the New Testament.

        1.) No commands to begin denominations are found in the New Testament.

        2.) Denominationalism is contrary to the unity for which Christ prayed and died (John 17:21; Eph. 2:14).

        3.) Whereas Christ sought to unite, through denominationalism men seek to divide.

    B. The English word *denominate* is taken from the Latin word *denominare* meaning "to name" or to "designate."

        1.) A "denomination" is a religious sect. Accordingly, to be "denominational" is to be sponsored by, or under the control of, some religious sect or sects.

        2.) "Denominationalism," therefore, is the division into such sects or denominations.[1]

        3.) Denominationalism is the re-forming and re-naming of churches to distinguish them from one another.

    C. The practice of distinguishing one group from another, with differing names, etc., was strictly condemned by Paul (1 Cor. 1:10-13).

    D. There is one body (Eph. 4:4; 1 Cor. 12:12).

        1.) The body of Christ is the church of Christ (Eph. 1:20-22).

        2.) By one Spirit are we all baptized into one body (1 Cor. 12:13).

II.   The church is not a social club.

    A. Emphasis must be given to the spiritual nature of the church over the social aspects of our relationships (1 Pet. 2:5).

    B. Christians are born again for the spiritual purpose of doing the Lord's work (Eph. 2:8-10).

    C. The parable of the life-saving station.[2]

---

[1] Noah Webster, *Webster's New Twentieth Century Dictionary*, ed. Jean L. McKechnie, 2nd ed., (Cleveland and New York: The World Publishing Co., 1995), 485.

[2] The parable of the life-saving station speaks of a life-saving station built upon the coast of treacherous waters by people who were rescued from those waters. In time, they added various amusements and lost focus of their original purpose. They ceased to be a life-saving station and became a social club. Souls continued to perish in the treacherous waters, while they ate, drank, and were merry. The parable speaks to the essential purpose and work of the church.

III. The church is not a private enterprise.
   A. Paul preached the gospel without charge (1 Cor. 9:18).
   B. The work of the church is funded by free-will offerings, not by charging for service rendered (1 Cor. 16:1-2; 2 Cor. 8-9).
   C. On the first visit our Savior made to Jerusalem during His earthly ministry, He condemned the Jews for making His house a house of merchandise (John 2:13-16). Also, on His final visit to Jerusalem, Jesus would rebuke for a second time this forbidden act (Matt. 21:12-13).
      1.) Merchandizing, in our English usage, simply means to buy, sell, or even to promote the sale of a product. The Jews had turned the temple into "a place where trade is carried on" or "a market house."[3]
      2.) The temple was a place of sacrifice, not financial gain. This is equally true of the church, which is the Lord's temple today (1 Cor. 3).
IV. The church is not a building.
   A. When Paul spoke of the church as the temple, he was not referring to a church building. He was referring to the people (1 Cor. 3:16-17; 6:19-20).

When a church loses its identity, it ceases to fulfill its spiritual purpose in the world.

[3] Joseph H. Thayer, *Thayer's Greek English Lexicon of the New Testament* (Peabody, MA: Hendrickson, 2002), 208.

- B. Christians must learn that they do not "go to church" but that they are "the church."
- C. The church is not a building of brick and mortar, but of living stones built upon one chief Cornerstone (1 Pet. 2:5-6).

V. The church is not a state-operated organization.
- A. State-operated systems of church government can be traced back to Constantine, Calvin and his followers, the followers of Luther, and King Henry VIII of England.
- B. The consequences of such an organization are evident in the outbreak of war and the occupation of foreign sovereignties.
  - 1.) In such cases, the borders of said church are spread through military might, as occupied sovereignties soon become oppressed by the religion of the conqueror.
  - 2.) Roman Catholic history is full of such conquests.
  - 3.) The borders of the Lord's church are expanded through the preaching of the gospel, not swords and spears (see Isa. 2:1-4).

VI. The church is not of human conception.
- A. God planned and prepared the church in heaven and placed the church on earth (2 Tim. 1:9-10).

        1.) The church did not begin with any preacher, movement, or creed.

        2.) The church is here according to the eternal purpose and wisdom of God (Eph. 3:10-11).

    B. Every denomination is of human origin. The Lord's church is of Divine origin.

VII. The church is not a replacement for a failed, earthly, and Jewish kingdom.

    A. The doctrine of premillennial dispensationalism is based upon the theory that the church was established as a temporary measure due to the Jews' rejection of Christ.

        1.) Of course, this would mean that His death was also not according to God's plan and was the result of Jewish rejection.

        2.) The Scriptures teach that His death and His church were planned before the foundation of the world (1 Pet. 1:19-20; Eph. 1:4).

    B. Jesus is now reigning on His throne in heaven (Acts 2:30-31; John 18:36).

VIII. The church is not a democracy;[4] it is a kingdom.[5]

---

[4] In some congregations a pure democracy is the trend. As such, there are no elders, no leaders, but everything is decided by congregational votes. Some evangelicals believe their churches are governed solely by the Holy Spirit, similar to the Quakers of old. Church members are instructed to be sensitive to the leading of the Holy Spirit, and thus any votes taken would be guided by Him.

    A. Christ is on His throne, governing His kingdom (Ps. 45:6-7; Heb. 1:8-9).

    B. His church is His kingdom (Heb. 12:22-28; Dan. 2:44).

        1.) The term *kingdom* denotes the government of the church.

        2.) The kingdom was established on the Day of Pentecost in the city of Jerusalem (Mark 9:1; Acts 1:8; Acts 2:1-4).

IX. The church is not an insignificant subject.

    A. Sadly, it is not uncommon to hear people express that they want a relationship with Christ without religion. Or, they want Christ but not the church.

    B. One cannot have Christ without the church.

        1.) He is Head over the body (Eph. 1:20-22).

---

[5] According to the writer of Hebrews (Heb. 12:22-23, 28), the church and the kingdom are one and the same. A series of questions will also help one to see that these two terms refer to the same institution. How does one come into the kingdom (John 3:3-5)? How does one come into the church (Acts 2:38)? Who is in the kingdom on earth that is not in the church? When did the kingdom begin (Mark 9:1; Acts 1:8; Acts 2:1-4)? When did the church begin (Acts 2:38-47)? Is any saved person outside of the kingdom (Col. 1:13)? Is any saved person outside of the church (Acts 2:47)? Who is head over the church (body) (Eph. 1:22-23)? Who is king over the kingdom (Heb. 1:8)? What law governs the church (1 Cor. 9:21)? What law governs the kingdom (Heb. 12:22-24)? Such questions teach us that one enters the kingdom the same way he enters the church. The same people who are in the kingdom are in the church. The kingdom began on the same day the church began. All saved people are in the kingdom. All saved people are in the church. Jesus is Head over the church and King over the kingdom. The same law governs both the kingdom and the church. Moreover, the kingdom and the church will be raised at the last day (1 Cor. 15:24; 1 Thess. 4:16-17). From such questions we can see that the Bible is not speaking of two separate groups of people but one and the same.

2.) He is the Savior of the body (Eph. 5:23).

Conclusion

I. In these first two lessons, effort has been given to distinguish the biblical nature of the Lord's church from the carnal nature of man-made churches.

II. One cannot overstate the importance of such a distinction.

   A. The church is now assembled on earth and will someday be assembled with Christ in heaven (1 Thess. 4:16-18; John 14:1-3).

   B. If a person desires to be in the Lord's heavenly assembly, he must enter the Lord's assembly while on earth.

III. Anyone can be added to this sacred assembly and spiritual kingdom by hearing the gospel preached (Rom. 10:17); believing the facts concerning Christ as revealed in the gospel (John 8:24); repenting of sin (2 Pet. 3:9); confessing faith in Christ (Rom. 10:9-10); and being baptized into Christ to wash away sins (Acts 22:16).

The Church in the Mystery of the Ages

Introduction

I. God's works were finished from the foundation of the world (Heb. 4:3). He declared the end from the beginning (Isa. 46:10).

   A. God determined the last day of His creation before the first day (Acts 17:31).

   B. God determined that He would send His Son as a sacrifice for our sins (Rev. 13:8; 1 Pet. 1:20-21).

   C. God prepared the gospel message before it was ever preached (2 Tim. 1:9).

   D. God ordained the fundamentals of the Christian faith before the foundation of the world (Eph. 1:4-6; 3:10-11).

   E. God prepared the kingdom of heaven before the foundation of the world (Matt. 25:34).

II. God has acted deliberately in every way imaginable to man to show man that His kingdom is here for a reason — an eternal purpose.

   A. Every aspect of the Christian religion is a matter of divine revelation and authority.

   B. It is not a mistake, a result of haphazard, last-minute planning or human innovation that we speak of the churches of Christ. Rather, it is because of God's infinite wisdom and eternal purpose to save man that He calls us out of the darkness of ignorance and sin and gathers us together into a spiritual body of believers, with His only Son seated as Head with all power and authority.

Discussion

I. What Is a Biblical Mystery?

    A. The word *mystery* is used in the New Testament to denote a subject or prophecy of old which needed further revelation or fulfillment for man to have a correct understanding.

        1.) Prior to such revelation, the subject's full meaning was "hidden" in the sense that complete understanding was not yet attained on the part of the hearer.

        2.) The word *mystery* is to be understood as a general that is executing his battle strategy. The general's strategy has been hidden, not yet fully revealed, until the time it was to be executed (cf. 1 Cor. 2:7-8; 4:1; Eph. 3:5).

    B. Matthew wrote of Jesus' use of parables by quoting Psalm 78:2, "I will open My mouth in parables; I will utter things which have been kept secret from the foundation of the world" (Matt. 13:35).

    C. Peter wrote, "Of this salvation the prophets have inquired and searched diligently, who prophesied of the grace that would come to you, searching what, or what manner of time, the Spirit of Christ who was in them was indicating when He testified beforehand the sufferings of Christ and the glories that would follow. To them it was revealed that, not to themselves, but to us they were ministering the things which now have been reported to you through those who have preached the gospel to you by the Holy Spirit sent from heaven – things which angels desire to look into" (1 Pet. 1:10-12).

1.) Peter understood that these Old Testament writers were writing by the inspiration of the Holy Spirit, for, "no prophecy of Scripture is of any private interpretation, for prophecy never came by the will of man, but holy men of God spoke as they were moved by the Holy Spirit" (2 Pet. 1:20-21).

2.) Peter also understood that he was communicating the answers to the prophecies for which the Old Testament heroes could only "desire to look into."

3.) Of the relationship between Old Testament prophecy and New Testament fulfillment, especially concerning Christ and His kingdom, Peter would say publicly to Jews at Jerusalem: "For Moses truly said to the fathers, 'The Lord your God will raise up for you a Prophet like me from your brethren. Him you shall hear in all things, whatever He says to you.

And it shall come to pass that every soul who will not hear that Prophet shall be utterly destroyed from among the people.' Yes, and all the prophets, from Samuel and those who follow, as many as have spoken, have also foretold these days" (Acts 3:22-24).

    D. To take these Old Testament prophecies concerning the kingdom and ignore their New Testament explanations is to abide in darkness, groping for, and yet gaining, no correct understanding.

        1.) We must live by that old adage, "The New Testament reveals what the Old Testament conceals."

        2.) And when the New Testament provides an explanation to an Old Testament prophecy, we ought to respect it as the intended purpose and fulfillment of that prophecy.

        3.) In other words, when we read, "This is that which was spoken by the prophet . . . " we ought not to be found saying, "But it could also mean . . . " God has given us the explanation by divine revelation and that should suffice.

II.   The Mystery of the Christ

    A. He would come from the seed of woman (Gen. 3:15; Isa. 7:14).

B. He would come through the family of Abraham (Gen. 12:3).
  C. He would come to make intercession for transgressors (Isa. 53).
  D. He would come and establish His government and kingdom (Isa. 9:6; Dan. 2:44).
  E. He did come and fulfill each of these prophecies (Matt. 1:20-23; see also Luke 1:32-33; 1Tim. 3:16).

III. The Mystery of Christ's Kingdom
  A. All nations of the earth were going to be blessed by Christ (Gen. 12:3).
    1.) Christ was going to be a light to the Gentiles (Isa. 49:6).
    2.) Paul explains that the fulfillment of these promises is in the church (Eph. 3:1-11).
    3.) Jews and Gentiles alike are saved and added by God to the kingdom of Christ through obedience to His gospel (Mark 16:15-16; Gal. 3:26-29).
    4.) God determined from the foundation of the world that the gospel would be preached to Jews and Gentiles alike, thus creating one new nation, a royal priesthood, a spiritual house built upon the one and only foundation of Jesus Christ His Son.
  B. According to God's eternal purpose, He spoke of the *eternal* kingdom.

1.) We read of this prophecy in Daniel 2:44, and we read that it has now been received in Hebrews 12:28.

2.) The church is that kingdom that shall stand forever.

C. A new name was to be given.

1.) It is by the manifold wisdom of God that this kingdom would be given a new name *after* the Gentiles should see His righteousness (Isa. 62:1-2; 65:15).

2.) The new name would signify an everlasting covenant (Isa. 61:8), and it would be an everlasting name (Isa. 56:5).

3.) In Acts chapter 10, we read of the first Gentile converts to Christ, and what do you suppose we find next but a new name being given – "And the disciples were first called Christians in Antioch" (Acts 11:26).

a.) Who was it that gave them this name? According to Isaiah, "The Gentiles shall see your righteousness, and all kings your glory. You shall be called by a new name, which the mouth of the Lord will name" (Isa. 62:2).

b.) The word "called" in Acts 11:26 literally means divinely called.

c.) Now, if it is true that the name "Christian" has been given by the manifold wisdom and eternal purpose of God and that it signifies an everlasting covenant God has made with His people — the church — by what wisdom and purpose do we have authority to call ourselves by any other name?

d.) And what covenant is signified by any other name?

e.) And in what other name is there salvation? "Nor is there salvation in any other, for there is no other name under heaven given among men by which we must be saved" (Acts 4:12).

f.) In what other name is there glory? God associates His glory with His name. Note, "I am the LORD, that is My name; and My glory I will not give to another, nor My praise to graven images" (Isa. 42:8); and again, "how should My name be profaned? And I will not give My glory to another" (Isa. 48:11); and lastly, "Therefore God also has highly exalted Him and given Him the name which is above every name, that at the name of Jesus every knee should bow, of those in heaven, and of those on earth, and of those under the earth, and that every tongue should confess that Jesus Christ is Lord, to the glory of God the Father" (Phil. 2:9-11).

4.) We call ourselves Christians, not because some man had an idea of what we should be called, but because of the eternal purpose of God, hidden throughout the ages, but now made known unto men in these last days. You can become a Christian as well. This too is according to the divine will and eternal purpose of God. He gave His Son to taste death for every man (Heb. 2:9).

D. The authority of Christ would prevail.

1.) God revealed Christ to the children of Israel through Moses saying, "I will raise up for them a Prophet like you from among their brethren, and will put My words in His mouth, and He shall speak to them all that I command Him. And it shall be that whoever will not hear My words, which He speaks in My name, I will require it of him" (Deut. 18:15-19).

a.) Jesus said of Himself, "For I have come down from heaven, not to do My own will, but the will of Him who sent Me" (John 6:38).

b.) And, "He who rejects Me, and does not receive My words, has that which judges him; the word that I have spoken will judge him in the last day" (John 12:48).

2.) God revealed to Jeremiah that a new covenant would be established in which He would remember our sins no more (Jer. 31:31-34).

    a.) The writer of Hebrews confirms, not only once but twice, that we now live under this covenant in Christ (Heb. 8:8 ff. and 10:16 ff.).

    b.) Moreover, the writer of Hebrews revealed that this covenant was established by the offering of the body of Christ — "once for all."

3.) God has made known to us that His Son would come with authority, that we should hearken unto His words, and that through His covenant we could be reconciled and forgiven completely.

4.) It is in the offering and covenant of Christ that Satan's head is crushed and the last enemy, which is death, is destroyed (1 Cor. 15:54; Heb. 2:14).

Conclusion

I. When one obeys the gospel, not only is he welcoming Christ as Savior, but he is also embracing the eternal purpose and manifold wisdom of God.

II. To refuse to hear Him who speaks (Heb. 12:25) is to abide in darkness of the devil and the futile foolishness of man.

The Establishment of the Church

Introduction

I. In this lesson we shall focus primarily upon the establishment of the Lord's church.

   A. By knowing when the Lord's church was established, we will know when the Lord's church was not established.

   B. Any church established at any other time could not be the Lord's church.

   C. This is the day that heaven and earth were wed together.

II. The church began in Jerusalem on the first Pentecost after our Lord's ascension into heaven.

   A. In Bible history, the Day of Pentecost is as pivotal as Moses on Sinai.

      1.) Pentecost — Feast of Weeks; held at the end of the wheat harvest in June — commemorated the giving of the Law.

      2.) Pentecost — 50th; 50 days from Passover; first day of the week; Jews assembled in Jerusalem from all around the world (Acts 2:5).

   B. Acts 2 has been correctly called the "hub of the Bible."

      1.) The Scriptures given before this day point to it.

      2.) The Scriptures given after this day reflect upon it (cf. Acts 11:15).

3.) Acts 2 teaches us about the unity and agreement of God's plan of salvation – (1) in heaven; (2) in scripture; and (3) among the saved.

Discussion

I.   Agreement in Heaven

    A. The Father made His presence known (Acts 2:1-3).

       1.) He did so when the Tabernacle was first erected in the wilderness (Ex. 40:33-35).

       2.) He did so when Solomon finished the Temple (1 Kings 8:10-13).

       3.) He did so on the Day of Pentecost when the church began.

    B. The Holy Spirit began His work as Comforter and Helper to the apostles (Acts 2:4).

       1.) Jesus foretold, "He will teach you all things, and bring to your remembrance all things that I said to you" (John 14:26).

       2.) And, "He will testify of Me" (John 15:26).

       3.) And, "He will guide you into all truth; for He will not speak on His own authority, but whatever He hears He will speak; and He will tell you things to come" (John 16:13).

       4.) The twelve spoke as the Spirit gave them utterance.

    C. The Lord Jesus acts for the first time as King upon His throne (Acts 2:30).

      1.) His first official act as King was to pardon 3,000 guilty souls.

      2.) Christ foretold this day.

          a.) He foretold the building of His church (Matt. 16:18-19).

          b.) He told of the coming kingdom through the power of the Spirit (Mark 9:1; Acts 1:8).

          c.) Jesus continued to teach of the coming kingdom before His ascension (Acts 1:3-6).

          d.) And He foretold that the preaching of the gospel would begin in Jerusalem (Luke 24:46-49).

II. Agreement in Scripture

    A. Peter directed the audience to the Scriptures as he spoke of Joel referring to the Holy Spirit (Joel 2:28-32).

      1.) He could have also quoted Isaiah or Micah (Isa. 2:2-3; Mic. 4:1-3). "Now it shall come to pass in the latter days That the mountain of the LORD's house Shall be established on the top of the mountains, And shall be exalted above the hills; And all nations shall flow to it. Many people shall come and say, 'Come, and let us go up to the mountain of the LORD, To the house of the God of Jacob; He will teach us His ways, And we shall walk in His paths.' For out of Zion shall go forth the law, And the word of the LORD from Jerusalem."

2.) He could have quoted Daniel (Dan. 2:44). "And in the days of these kings the God of heaven will set up a kingdom which shall never be destroyed; and the kingdom shall not be left to other people; it shall break in pieces and consume all these kingdoms, and it shall stand forever."[1]

B. On Pentecost, Peter spoke of David with reference to Christ upon His throne (Ps. 16:8-10; 110:1).

1.) He could have also quoted Jeremiah (Jer. 3:17). "At that time Jerusalem shall be called The Throne of the LORD, and all the nations shall be gathered to it, to the name of the LORD, to Jerusalem. No more shall they follow the dictates of their evil hearts."

2.) He could have also quoted Zechariah (Zech. 6:12-13). "Thus says the Lord of hosts, saying: 'Behold, the Man whose name *is* the BRANCH! From His place He shall branch out, And He shall build the temple of the Lord; Yes, He shall build the temple of the Lord. He shall bear the glory, And shall sit

---

[1] The kings foretold by Daniel were the kings (Caesars) of Rome. Rome was the fourth world empire from Babylon — in order, Babylon, Medo-Persia, Greece, and Rome. The kingdom of God would be established in the day of the Roman Empire. After Pentecost, the apostles preached the established kingdom (Acts 8:12; 14:22; 19:8; 20:25; 28:23; 28:31). Paul taught how Christ's blood had bought the church (Acts 20:28). Paul taught of those who were taken from darkness and added to the kingdom (Col. 1:13). The writer of Hebrews taught the kingdom had been received (Heb. 12:28).

   and rule on His throne; So He shall be a priest on His throne, And the counsel of peace shall be between them both.'"

  C. All of this shows that what happened to Christ was according to the determinate counsel and foreknowledge of God (Acts 2:23).

III. Agreement Among the Saved

  A. They heard the same plan of salvation (Acts 2:37-39).

   1.) Peter was not telling people to be baptized for the forgiveness of sins, while John was telling people to say a "Sinner's Prayer," or James was having babies sprinkled with water.

   2.) One message was taught, heard, and obeyed from Acts 2 to Revelation 22.

  B. They obeyed the same way (Acts 2:40-41).

  C. They followed the same doctrine and worshipped the same way (v.42).

  D. They saw to the needs of one another with gladness and singleness of heart (vv.44-46).

  E. They grew together spiritually and numerically (v.47).

Conclusion

I. One religion was authorized by heaven to occupy the earth.

II. Only one religion can claim the same agreement in heaven, in scripture, and among the saved. Let us return to the principles taught this day and have that same agreement

The Kingdom and the Church (1)

Introduction

I. The church is spoken of with three distinctions in the New Testament.

   A. The church is a body with reference to its organization.

      1.) Christ is the Head of this body (Eph. 1:22-23).

      2.) Individual Christians are members of one another (1 Cor. 12:12, 20, 27).

   B. The church is "called out" — *ekklesia* — pertaining to its relationship with the world (1 Pet. 2:9).

      1.) It is separate and distinct from the world (2 Cor. 6:17).

         a.) The church is separate from the world in its ideals, values, worldview, view of God, view of man, view of right and wrong, ethics, morals, and virtues.

         b.) The Christian is also separate from the former man, the person he used to be (1 Cor. 6:11; Eph. 2:1 ff.).

      2.) Christians are called out from the world by the preaching of the gospel (2 Thess. 2:14).

   C. The church is a kingdom regarding its government.

      1.) Christ is the King.

      2.) His law is the constitution.

II. The matter of the church being a kingdom is the issue we shall study over the next two lessons.

    A. Here is a matter of utmost importance.

    B. All accountable souls are either in the kingdom of Satan (Matt. 12:26), which is the kingdom of darkness, or they are in the kingdom of God's dear Son (Col. 1:13).

Discussion

I. The Church of Christ Is the Kingdom of Christ.

    A. In the church we find the government (rule and law) of Christ (Isa. 9:6-7).[1]

    B. His law, like His kingdom, was established by His death and resurrection (Heb. 9:15-16).

        1.) No one was under the law of Christ until Pentecost when the gospel was preached in its fullness for the first time.

        2.) No one was in the kingdom of Christ until Pentecost when the door was opened with Peter's sermon (Matt. 16:18-19).

    C. A government cannot exist without a law. A law cannot exist without a government.

---

[1] The word *kingdom* describes the government of the church. T.W. Brents observed, "As respects law, the church is truly a *kingdom* – an *absolute monarchy*. All its laws emanate from the King, and its subjects have no part in making them. There is no *representative democracy* connected with it. No council, convention, or legislative assembly has power or authority to abolish, alter, or amend them. It is a *kingdom*, not a *republic*." T.W. Brents, *The Gospel Plan of Salvation* (Bowling Green, KY: Guardian of Truth Foundation, 1987), 118.

        1.) The law and the kingdom of Christ began at the same time.

        2.) The kingdom was established on Pentecost and the law was proclaimed first in Jerusalem (Isa. 2:1-4; Luke 24:44-47; Acts 2:1-42).

    D. The church/kingdom consists of those who have obeyed the Lord, been redeemed by the Lord, and been separated by the Lord unto Himself from the world.

    E. Christ turns sinners into kings and priests when He washes them in His own blood (Rev. 1:5-6).

        1.) The kingdom is made up of born-again people (John 3:3-5).

        2.) When a person is born again, he enters the kingdom. He enters the church (Acts 2:38-41, 47).

II. The Church of Christ is the Realm of Christ.

    A. A *realm* is a royal jurisdiction or extent of government.[2]

        1.) What is the jurisdiction of Christ or the extent of His government?

        2.) To be sure, it is not geographical; it is not of this world (John 18:36).

        3.) The church is a spiritual kingdom.

        4.) He reigns within the Spirit of every faithful Christian.

---

[2] Webster, *Webster's Dictionary*.

        5.) The church cannot be established, or the religion of Christ propagated, by force (Matt. 11:12; Isa. 2:4).
   B. The borders of the kingdom are spread as souls are freely converted to Him (Matt. 11:28-30; Rev. 22:17).
        1.) Man is added to this kingdom upon obedience to His word (Luke 8:11).
        2.) Man can also close the kingdom to others by false doctrines, deception, and diabolical schemes used to supplant His word (Matt. 23:13).
        3.) Once in the kingdom, man must live according to the law of the King and must never look back (Luke 9:62).
        4.) Only those who obey the Lord can rightfully call Him "Lord" (Luke 6:46).
        5.) The souls who honor and obey Christ as Lord comprise His royal jurisdiction.

III. The Church of Christ is the Dominion of Christ.
   A. To speak of the dominion of Christ is to refer to those who are governed by Christ.
        1.) Not everyone chooses to be governed by Christ (2 Thess. 1:8).
        2.) Not everyone who claims to be governed by Christ is truly obedient to Him (Matt. 7:21-23).
   B. The church is the body of Christ (1 Cor. 12:13).

C. The church is the house, or family of the Lord, where His children can be found (1 Tim. 3:15; Gal. 3:26-27; Rom. 8:15-16).

D. The church is the vineyard of the Lord (Matt. 13:3-9; 18-23).

E. The church is the temple of the Lord (1 Cor. 3:9 ff.).

F. The church consists of the people who are faithful in Christ Jesus (Eph. 1:1).

Conclusion

I. The kingdom on earth is His church.

II. The kingdom in eternity is heaven (Matt. 25:34).

III. To live in the kingdom in eternity, one must live in the kingdom on earth (John 3:3-5).

The Kingdom and the Church (2)

Introduction

I. In the previous lesson on this subject, we discussed the biblical nature of the Lord's church as pertaining to its government.

    A. The church is a kingdom.

    B. The New Testament is its law.

II. In this lesson, we will give attention to three false doctrines concerning the kingdom of Christ.

    A. It should be our desire to know the truth and teach the truth on any biblical subject.

    B. We should desire to do so because of a desire to honor and obey God.

Discussion

I. Premillennial Dispensationalism

    A. The doctrine of premillennial dispensationalism places the establishment of the kingdom in the future after the second coming of Christ.[1]

    B. According to this teaching the kingdom and the church are not the same institution.

        1.) They believe the church was established as a temporary substitute for the kingdom due to Israel's rejection of the Messiah.

---

[1] R. H. Boll, *The Kingdom of God* (Louisville, KY: Word and Work, n.d.), 13.

- 2.) They believe Jesus was coming to make a world empire and military power out of Israel, but because He was rejected, He established the church instead of His kingdom.
- 3.) Premillennialists make the same mistake the Jews made and are making. They are looking for the Messiah to establish an earthly kingdom.

C. The doctrine asserts:
- 1.) Jesus will reign on the throne of David in Jerusalem for 1,000 years.
- 2.) The temple in Jerusalem will be rebuilt.
- 3.) The Levitical priesthood will be restored.
- 4.) The distinction between Jews and Gentiles will again be apparent.

D. Answering these assertions:
- 1.) Jesus came into this world knowing He would be despised and rejected (Isa. 53:3; Acts 2:23; Rev. 13:8).
- 2.) The only ones unaware of God's plan were the Jews (1 Cor. 2:8).
- 3.) Jesus' kingdom is not of this world (John 6:15; 18:36).
- 4.) Jesus is now reigning on His throne in heaven (Acts 2:29-36; Acts 5:31; Heb. 1:8-9).

5.) His throne was never going to be in Jerusalem (Jer. 22:30; Matt. 1:11).

6.) His kingdom now exists (Col. 1:13; Heb. 12:28).

7.) His priesthood will never be replaced (Heb. 7:24).

8.) In His kingdom there is no discrimination between Jews and Gentiles (Mark 16:15-16; Rom. 1:16-17; Gal. 3:26-29).

9.) When Jesus returns, it will be to gather His kingdom from the earth, not to establish His kingdom upon the earth (1 Thess. 4:13-18; Heb. 9:28; 2 Pet. 3:10-13).

II. During the Ministry of John the Baptist

A. Some place the establishment of the kingdom during the ministry of John the Baptist.[2]

1.) If this is in fact the case, and the kingdom began with John, why was John not in the kingdom (see Matt. 11:11)?

2.) If the kingdom was established during the days of John the Baptist, the apostles did not know it. They asked Jesus before His ascension "Lord, will You at this time restore the kingdom to Israel?" (Acts 1:6)

3.) Moreover, if the kingdom began during the days of John, Jesus did not know it. He refused to partake of

---

[2] Baptists used to maintain this doctrine zealously. The Missionary Baptist debater Ben M. Bogard argued against N.B. Hardeman, E. M. Borden, and W. Curtis Porter that the kingdom/church began during the days of John the Baptist.

the supper with the twelve "until the kingdom of God shall come" (Luke 22:18; cf. 1 Cor. 11:23; Acts 20:7).

    B. Both John and Jesus preached, "Repent, for the kingdom of heaven is at hand."

        1.) They did not say it was "already."

        2.) That clarion voice crying in the wilderness said it was "at hand."

        3.) Jesus even said it was "nigh at hand" (Luke 21:31).

    C. John the Baptist had already been killed (Matt. 14:10-12) when Jesus said, "upon this rock I will build My church" and that Peter would receive the "keys to the kingdom" (Matt. 16:18-19).

III. The Kingdom Has Always Existed

    A. Others believe the kingdom has always been present upon the earth in different manifestations.[3]

    B. We agree that the earth has never been without God as its divine Ruler.

        1.) God is the Judge of all the earth (Gen. 18:25).

        2.) He is the great King over all the earth (Ps. 47:2; 103:19, 22).

        3.) See also 2 Chron. 36:22-23; Ezra 1:1; Dan. 4:34-35; 6:25-26.

---

[3] Everett Ferguson, *The New Testament Church*, 3rd ed. (Abilene, TX: ACU Press, 2008), 85. R. H. Boll believed this as well. See *Kingdom of God*, 7.

C. The Old Testament also speaks of a kingdom to come, which would be established by Christ (Isa. 9:6-8; Dan. 2:44; 7:13-14).
   1.) Upon His ascension into heaven, He was crowned (Heb. 2:9) and coronated (Heb. 1:8-9) as Lord and Christ (Acts 2:36).
   2.) He was given all authority in heaven and earth (Matt. 28:18-20).
   3.) He has power/authority over the devil to destroy the works of the devil and to cast him into outer darkness (Heb. 2:14; Rev. 20:10).
   4.) His rule was established over all things.
      a.) Yet, one should not believe the devil is in the kingdom of God simply because he will be subjected to the rule of God.
      b.) All men will ultimately submit to the will of God (Rom. 14:10-11).
      c.) But all men do not now submit to the will of God.
      d.) Only those who submit to His will in this life are born again and enter His kingdom (John 3:3-5).
F. John the Baptist was under the *rule* of God but was not in the promised kingdom.
   1.) The same could be said for the faithful in the Old Testament.

  2.) Submitting to the rule of God could only add a person to the kingdom of God once it had been established on the earth.

  3.) Christ had to be given the key to the house of David (Isa. 22:22; 2 Sam. 7:12-17) for the doors of the family of God to be opened to include the Gentiles (Isa. 49:6; 62:2; Eph. 2:13-16).

   a.) It was not until the church was established that the doors were opened and His rule commenced.

   b.) A new and living way was inaugurated (Heb. 10:20).

   c.) One new man was created (Eph. 2:15-16).

   d.) A new covenant became law (Heb. 8:7-13).

  5.) When He returns, He will gather His kingdom (Matt. 13:3-9; 18-23) and deliver it to the Father (1 Cor.15:25-26; Phil. 2:5-8).

Conclusion

I. The kingdom on earth is His church.

II. The kingdom in eternity is heaven (Matt. 25:34).

III. To live in the kingdom in eternity, one must live in the kingdom on earth (John 3:3-5).

The Rule of Faith and Practice for the Church

Introduction

I. God has given a rule of faith and practice for the church (Phil. 3:16; 1 Cor. 1:10).

II. No congregation is at liberty to establish their own set of rules (another gospel) to differ from the body of Christ at large (Gal. 1:6-9; 2 John 9-11; Eph. 4:1-6).

III. The way to religious unity is to learn and uphold the rule of faith and practice which God has given to man.

    A. If we walk by the same rule, we will be minding the same thing (Phil. 3:16-17).

    B. Anyone who does otherwise is an enemy of the cross of Christ (Phil. 3:18; Eph. 2:13-16).

Discussion

I. What Is the Rule of Faith and Practice for the Church?

    A. Is it based upon man's opinion?

        1.) The way of man is not in himself (Jer. 10:23).

        2.) Man is not saved by self-revelation or personal feelings.

        3.) Just because something seems right does not mean that it is right (Prov. 14:12).

        4.) We must not use each other as a standard for our faith (1 Cor. 4:6; 2 Cor. 10:12)

    B. Is it based upon man's traditions?

1.) Consider the harm man-made traditions caused in Christ's day (Matt. 15:1-9; Mark 7:1-13).
   a.) Traditions make void the word of God (Mark 7:13).
   b.) Traditions cause religious ignorance (Matt. 15:2; Mark 7:1-5).
   c.) Traditions cause men to be separated from God (Matt. 15:3).
   d.) Traditions cause hearts to be far from God (Matt. 15:8).
   e.) Traditions cause vain worship (Matt. 15:9).
   f.) Traditions cause men to be rooted up (Matt. 15:13).
2.) Traditions also cause men to be spoiled in philosophy and vain deceit (Col. 2:8).
   a.) So often the gospel of Christ is being replaced by human philosophy.
   b.) Such is vain deceit.
C. Is it based upon wrongful interpretations of the Scriptures?
   1.) Twisting of the Scriptures leads to the destruction of the soul (2 Pet. 3:15-16).
      a.) A wrongful interpretation will cause one to be unstable and unlearned.

        b.) A wrongful interpretation could lead to certain destruction in hell.
- D. Is it to be based upon man's popular vote?
    - 1.) What is popular is not always right and what is right is not always popular (Matt. 7:13-14).
    - 2.) The majority wanted to crucify Jesus (Matt. 27:15-26). Were they right?
- E. Is the rule of faith and practice in fact the word of God?
    - 1.) Only the Scriptures are given by God's inspiration and they are all we need for doctrine and every good work (2 Tim. 3:16-17).
    - 2.) The word of God is the only thing we are commanded to preach (2 Tim. 4:1-4).
    - 3.) The word of God is the only thing we are commanded to study (John 5:39; 2 Tim. 2:15).
    - 4.) The word of God is the only word by which we shall be judged (John 12:48).

II. How Does One Learn of the Faith and Practice God Commands?
- A. Diligently study the word of God (John 5:39).
- B. Rightly divide the word (2 Tim. 2:15).
    - 1.) The Old Testament is meant for our learning (Rom. 15:4).
    - 2.) The New Testament is meant for our keeping (Heb. 2:1-4).

        3.) God took away the first that He might establish the second (Heb. 10:9).

        4.) Christ is the end of the law (Rom. 10:4).

    C. When you come to know and understand the truth, obey it! (Heb. 5:8-9)

III. How Does One Uphold the Faith and Practice of the Church?

    A. Earnestly contend for it (Jude 3).

    B. Speak the truth in love (Eph. 4:15).

    C. Answer with meekness and respect (1 Pet. 3:15).

    D. Answer with knowledge and humility (2 Tim. 2:23-26).

    E. Answer emphasizing either compassion or fear (Jude 22; 2 Cor. 5:10, 11).

    F. Answer logically from the Scriptures (Acts 17:2).

    G. Exhort and convince the gainsayers (Titus 1:9).

Conclusion

I. How can man know if he is pleasing God in his teachings and by his works?

    A. Only by faith can we please God (Heb. 11:6).

    B. The only way to walk by faith is to walk by the word of God (Rom. 10:17).

II. We must go to the word of God, and the word of God alone, for our teachings and our practices.

III. Nothing more than, less than, or other than this will do!

The Church in Infancy and Maturity

Introduction

I. The first century church had certain gifts and offices not applicable to the church in coming generations.

   A. Such gifts and offices distinguish the church in infancy and maturity.

   B. Such is the point of Paul's statement in 1 Corinthians 13:11 – "When I was a child, I spoke as a child, I understood as a child, I thought as a child; but when I became a man, I put away childish things."

II. The distinction to be made is crucial due to the claims of charismatics, false teachers, false prophets, and cultists.

   A. The claim of supernatural ability and revelation has caused countless superstitious and has enabled unlearned souls to be misguided and manipulated by devilish perpetrators in sheep's clothing.

   B. Paul dealt with false apostles and prophets in his day and so too must we (2 Cor. 11:13).

Discussion

I. Offices Held Only by the Infant Church (1 Cor. 12:28)

   A. The Apostles

      1.) Apostles were set apart by Christ.

         a.) The original twelve (Matt. 10:1-4)

         b.) Judas' replacement (Acts 1:15-26)

         c.) Paul was born out of due time (1 Cor. 15:5-8).

      2.) Apostles were eyewitness of His resurrection (Acts 1:22).

      3.) Apostles were able to pass along spiritual gifts (Acts 8:14-17; Rom. 1:11-12; 1 Cor. 9:1-2).

      4.) Paul was the last the apostle (1 Cor. 15:8).

      5.) The ability to pass along spiritual gifts ended with the apostles.

B. The Prophets

      1.) Prophets were inspired teachers in the early church (Eph. 4:11).

      2.) Prophets received their inspiration through the laying on of the apostles' hands (1 Cor. 12:10).

          a.) Without apostles, there could be no prophets.

          b.) With the completion of God's revealed word, there is no need for these inspired prophets (Eph. 4:13).

          c.) The Scriptures completely furnish the church with doctrine (2 Tim. 3:16-17).

          d.) Consider the wisdom of God and the benefit of forever recording His word on a printed page:

                1.) A book serves as an accurate recording of the people, places, events, statements, and facts of the matter.

                2.) A book can be read, re-read, and studied.

3.) A book can be accurately translated into different languages.

4.) A book can serve to verify the truthfulness of the preacher's claims and doctrine.

3.) 1 Cor. 14:37 – "If anyone thinks himself to be a prophet or spiritual, let him acknowledge that the things which I write to you are the commandments of the Lord."

4.) Test the modern-day prophets to see if what they prophesy comes to pass (Deut. 18:22).

5.) Test the modern-day dreamer of dreams to see if his revelation is consistent with the word (Deut. 13:1-5; 2 Thess. 2).

II. Gifts Possessed Only by the Infant Church (1 Cor. 12:1-11)

A. The purpose for these gifts:

1.) To teach the word (2 Pet. 1:20-21)

2.) To confirm the word (Mark 16:20; Heb. 2:4)

B. These gifts were bestowed by the laying on of the apostles' hands (Acts 8:18; Rom. 1:11; 1 Cor.9:1-2; 2 Tim.1:6).

C. To distinguish between the nature of biblical miracles and so-called miracles being performed today, one needs only to compare the biblical accounts with the accounts of today.

1.) Biblical miracles were unquestionably miraculous.

  2.) Biblical miracles provided true healing for any condition.

  3.) Biblical miracles were immediate and complete.

  4.) Biblical miracles could affect nature.

  5.) Biblical miracles could even raise the dead.

 D. When did these miracles cease?

  1.) When the apostles died, no one remained with the ability to pass along such supernatural gifts.

  2.) God had already completed His revelation by that time, thus making the office of the inspired prophet obsolete.

III. Some Things that Did Not Cease

 A. Jesus remains the Head and Savior of the church (Eph. 1:20-22; 5:23; Heb. 10:14; 13:8).

 B. God's word is still the rule of faith and practice for the church (Jude 3).

 C. Mankind remains obligated to obey God's word and yield to Christ's will to receive salvation (Matt. 28:18-20; Heb. 5:9).

Conclusion

I. The early church had peculiar offices and gifts that were to cease (1 Cor. 13:8-10).

II. We must seek those things which abide rather than desire that which has ceased (1 Cor. 13:13).

The Structure of the Church Universal

Introduction

I. No man, council, denomination, congregation, or creed should ever seek to usurp, supplant, or substitute the authority Christ has over His church – in any way.

   A. Concerning creeds: "None of these creeds, whether Catholic or Protestant, tells a man how to become a Christian. They tell a man how he may become a Catholic, a Lutheran, a Reformer, an Episcopalian, a Presbyterian, a Methodist, a Baptist, perchance. There is not a Confession of Faith in existence that ever saved a soul. As human compositions, one is just as full of light and knowledge as another, and just as efficacious in the salvation of the soul. They all originated in the councils of men; they were digested in the heat of human passions; they were concocted and planned by envious and rival theologians; they became the symbols – the insignia – of rival princes; they have always engendered strife, hatred, malice, bigotry, intolerance and persecution, and will continue to do so until the end of time. There is no Christian love in them; there is nothing in them that will unite the people of God and make them one people. The mind of God is not found in them, and the spirit of Christ does not breathe through them. They confuse the human mind; they divide the counsels of Christians;

they paralyze the power of truth; they make a fable of the gospel; they mock the prayers of the Savior; they make void the law of God; they infuse the spirit of sectarianism; they cramp the human intellect; they place insuperable barriers between those seeking love and unity upon the basis of the Bible."[1]

    B. "Creeds began at the very point where reformation ceased."[2]

II.   The study of Christ's authority to His church is THE KEY to understanding the structure of the New Testament church.

    A. The structure of the church is both universal (referring to the body of Christ at large) and local (pertaining to the various independent congregations which comprise the body of Christ).

    B. In this lesson we will be studying the structure of the church in the universal sense of the phrase.

III.   To come to a better understanding of the structure of the Lord's church in a universal sense, we must study various relationships involved.

Discussion

I.   Christ's Relationship with His Church

    A. He is the Savior of the Church (Eph. 5:23; Acts 20:28).

---

[1] John F. Rowe, *History of Reformatory Movements*, (Indianapolis, IN: Faith and Facts Publishing Co., 1993), 51—52.
[2] Rowe, 44.

B. He is the Builder of the Church (Matt. 16:18; Heb. 8:1-2).
C. He is the Foundation of the Church (1 Cor. 3:11).
D. He is the Head of the Church (Eph. 1:20-23; Col. 1:18).
E. His word is the sole Authority for the Church (Matt. 28:28; Acts 2:36; Col. 3:17).
   1.) Man is never commanded to obey the doctrines of men. But he is commanded to obey the word of Christ (Matt. 17:5; John 14:15; 15:10, 14; Luke 6:46; Matt. 7:21-27).
   2.) Man will not be judged by any doctrine or commandment of men. But he will be judged by the word of Christ (John 12:48).
   3.) A man could take every creed book ever written and throw it in the trash and obey only the word of God, and he would be saved eternally.
   4.) Only Christ has the authority to command, forgive, judge, and welcome into heaven eternal.
II. The Church's Relationship with Christ
A. Every individual Christian must be submissive to Christ (James 4:6-10).
   1.) Subject to Him to become a Christian (Luke 24:7)
   2.) Subject to Him to live as a Christian (John 10:27-28)

B. Collectively, each congregation must be submissive to Christ (Rev. 2-3).
　1.) Christ is over His house (Heb. 3:1-6).
　2.) Christ is our Chief Shepherd (John 10:11-16; Heb. 13:20-21; 1 Pet. 2:25; 1 Pet. 5:4).
C. The church can never be subject to another, or through another, and remain true to Christ (1Tim. 2:5; 1 John 2:1-2).

III. Congregational Relationships within the Church Universal
A. The church (in the collective sense) is comprised of many independent, autonomous congregations.
　1.) Every congregation is to be self-governed.
　2.) Concerning the churches of Christ as they existed in the first century, the overwhelming testimony of church history has been succinctly stated by the venerable church historian John Lawrence Mosheim, "The churches of those early times were entirely independent; and none of them subject to any foreign jurisdiction, but each was governed by its own rulers and its own laws. For, though the churches founded by the apostles had the particular deference shown them, that they were consulted in difficult cases, yet they had no judicial authority, no fort of supremacy over the others, nor the least right to enact laws for them. Nothing, on the contrary, is

more evident than the perfect equality that reigned among primitive churches; nor does there even appear, in the first century, the smallest trace of that association of provincial churches, from which councils and metropolitans derive their origin."[3]

3.) He continues: "There reigned among the members of the Christian Church, however distinguished they were by worldly rank and titles, not only an amiable harmony but also a perfect equality . . . Nor, in this first century, was the distinction made between Christians of a more or less perfect order, which took place . . . The rulers of the church were called either presbyters or bishops, which two titles are, in the New Testament, undoubtedly applied to the same order of men."[4]

4.) Thus, "Such was the constitution of the Christian Church in its infancy, when its assemblies were neither numerous nor splendid. Three or four presbyters, men of remarkable piety and wisdom, ruled these small congregations in perfect harmony, nor did they stand in need of any president or superior to maintain concord and order where no dissentions were known . . . Let none, however, confound the

---

[3] John Lawrence Mosheim, *Ecclesiastical History*, vol.1, (Rosemead, CA: Old Paths Book Club, 1959), 86.
[4] Mosheim, 81.

bishops of this primitive and golden period of the church with those with those of whom we read in the following ages . . . A bishop during the first and second centuries was a person who had the care of one Christian assembly, which at the time, was, generally speaking, small enough to be contained in a private house."[5]

      5.) It took men hundreds of years and many councils to change the beauty and simplicity of God's original program for the church.

  B. No congregation has ever been set over another congregation.

      1.) The elders at Ephesus were the overseers and feeders of that flock, not of any other flock (Acts 20:28).

      2.) Each congregation is to be self-governing (Acts 14:23).

      3.) We have fellowship with one another because we have fellowship in Christ (1 Cor. 1:9).

      4.) All relationships stem from the relationship a church has with Christ.

  C. Congregations can work together (Acts 11:27-30; Romans 15:25-26).

  D. Congregations can choose not to work together.

---

[5] Mosheim, 85-86.

1.) No congregation can force another congregation in any way.
2.) If a good work turns sour, a congregation can cease support.
3.) Apostasy and sectarianism are limited by God's design of congregational autonomy.
4.) In God's plan of church organization, there is nothing larger than or smaller than the local church.

Conclusion

I. Does any of this matter?
II. Man has always been instructed not to go beyond the boundaries of divine revelation (Deut. 4:2; 1 Cor. 4:6; 2 Cor. 10:12; Rev. 22:18-19).
III. It is not for man to change the word of God, but for the word of God to change man.

The Structure of the Local Church

Introduction

I. The church is the assembly of all who have been called out of sin by obedience to the gospel (Col. 1:13; 1 Pet. 2:9).

II. The Lord's assembly is comprised of autonomous, independent, and individual congregations.

III. In this lesson we shall focus on the structure and responsibilities of such congregations.

Discussion

I. Leadership

   A. The organization and government for the church has been provided by God.

      1.) Such an organization consists of independent, local congregations being overseen by a group of elders.[1]

      2.) The minister facilitates in the teaching of the gospel, and the deacons assists in serving the congregation.

      3.) Each congregation is made up of men and women who have obeyed the gospel and have been added to the church by God Himself (Acts 2:42, 47).

---

[1] In the biblical sense of the word *pastor,* the words *elder*, *bishop*, *overseer*, and *shepherd* are synonymous. The pastor and the evangelist clearly had two different positions in the early church. In the New Testament, a bishop was one of the elders, pastors, or overseers of a local congregation (cf. Acts 14:23). Qualifications for this office are found in 1 Tim. 3:1-7.

B. Elders are to be ordained in every congregation (Acts 14:23). The qualifications for elders are found in the Bible (1Tim. 3; Titus 1). The work of the elders is also found in the Scriptures. These men are to feed and oversee the flock (Acts 20:28; Heb 13:7, 17; 1 Pet. 5:2-3). They are to guard against "wolves" and "gainsayers" – shepherding the flock as examples and not as lords of God's heritage. They are to look to the Chief Shepherd, Christ Jesus, as an example in all things (1 Pet. 5:4).

C. The following New Testament passages show that the will of God is for a plurality of elders to oversee each local church:

1.) "And when they had ordained them **elders** in every church, and had prayed with fasting, they commended **them** to the Lord, on whom **they** believed" (Acts 14:23).

2.) "Take heed therefore unto **yourselves**, and to all the flock, over the which the Holy Ghost hath made you **overseers**, to feed the church of God, which he hath purchased with his own blood" (Acts 20:28).

3.) "And the day following Paul went in with us unto James; and all the **elders** were present" (Acts 21:18).

4.) "Paul and Timotheus, the servants of Jesus Christ, to all the saints in Christ Jesus which are at Philippi, with the **bishops** and deacons" (Phil. 1:1).

5.) "For this cause left I thee in Crete, that thou shouldest set in order the things that are wanting, and ordain **elders** in every city, as I had appointed thee" (Titus 1:5).

6.) "Remember **them** which have the rule over you, who have spoken unto you the word of God: whose faith follow, considering the end of **their** conversation" (Heb. 13:7).

7.) "Obey **them** that have the rule over you, and submit yourselves: for **they** watch for your souls, as **they** that must give account, that **they** may do it with joy, and not with grief: for that is unprofitable for you" (Heb. 13:17).

8.) "Is any sick among you? let him call for the **elders** of the church; and let **them** pray over him, anointing him with oil in the name of the Lord" (James 5:14).

9.) "The **elders** which are among you I exhort, who am also an elder, and a witness of the sufferings of Christ, and also a partaker of the glory that shall be revealed" (1 Pet. 5:1).

D. Deacons

        1.) Deacons are servants in the local church and the work of the church.

        2.) The qualifications for deacons are also found in the Bible (1 Tim. 3:8-13).

        3.) The things that qualify the man should also disqualify him. A congregation should never have elders and deacons just to say they have them.

    E. Preachers

        1.) Note the qualifications (2 Tim. 2:2).

            a.) "Faithful men" are required.

            b.) Women are not to be elders, deacons, or preachers (1 Cor. 14:34 ff; 1 Tim. 2:11 ff).

            c.) Unfaithful men should not be preachers.

        2.) Note the responsibilities (1 Pet. 4:11).

        3.) Note the pay scale (1 Cor. 9:7-14, 18).

            a.) Gospel preachers should not "charge" for their preaching (v.18).

            b.) The church should take care of their preachers according to their needs (vv.7-14).

II. Membership

    A. Note the terms of admission (Acts 2:38-41).

    B. Note the terms of membership (Acts 2:42; 2 Tim. 2:19; 1 John 2:6).

    C. Congregational responsibilities include:

        1.) Encouragement (Heb. 10:24)

2.) Conflict management and discipline (Matt. 18:15-17; 1 Cor. 5)

   a.) Withdraw from the immoral brother (1 Cor. 5).

   b.) Withdraw from the divisive brother (Titus 3:10).

   c.) Withdraw from the disorderly brother (2 Thess. 3:6).

   d.) Withdraw from the false teacher (Rom. 16:17-18).

3.) Submit to biblical elders (Heb. 13:17).

4.) Support to those who labor in the ministry (Gal. 6:6).

5.) Maintain good work (1 Cor. 15:58).

6.) Worship in spirit and truth (John 4:21-24).

III. Fellowship

A. Fellowship is more than a meal.

B. Fellowship describes the relationship we have with one another as Christians (1 John 1:3).

C. "One Another" Passages

   1.) <u>Love</u> one another (John 13:34, 35; 15:12, 17; Rom. 13:8; 1 Thess. 3:12, 4:9; 1 Pet. 1:22; 1 John 3:11, 23, 4:7, 11, 12; 2 John 5).

   2.) Be <u>kindly affectionate</u> one to another …. in honor <u>preferring</u> one another (Rom. 12:10).

   3.) Be <u>of the same mind</u> one toward another (Rom. 12:16).

4.) <u>Edify</u> one another (Rom. 14:19). This same truth is revealed in Eph. 4:16.

5.) <u>Admonish</u> one another (Rom. 15:14; Col. 3:16).

6.) <u>Salute</u> or <u>greet</u> one another (Rom. 16:16; 1 Cor. 16:20; 2 Cor. 13:12; 1 Pet. 5:14).

   a.) <u>Serve</u> one another (Gal. 5:13).

   b.) <u>Bear the burdens</u> of one another (Gal. 6:2).

   c.) <u>Forbearing</u> and <u>forgiving</u> one another (Eph. 4:2; Col. 3:13).

   d.) <u>Be kind</u> one to another (Eph. 4:32).

   e.) <u>Submit</u> one to another (Eph. 5:21; 1 Pet. 5:5).

   f.) <u>Lie not</u> one to another (Col. 3:9), rather, <u>speak truth</u> one to another (Eph. 4:25), not evil (James 4:11).

   g.) <u>Comfort</u> one another (1 Thess. 4:18).

   h.) <u>Compassion</u> for one another (1 Pet. 3:8-9).

   i.) <u>Grudge not</u> one against another (James 5:9).

   j.) <u>Confess faults</u> one to another (James 5:16).

7.) From these passages we see what it means to consider one another in the way God intends.

8.) We cannot be living faithfully unless we are treating each other properly.

Conclusion

I. Every member in the local congregation is important to the overall health of the church.

II. Each member has qualifications and responsibilities.
III. A church that pleases God is a church that is qualified for service takes its responsibilities seriously.

The Worship of the Church

Introduction

I. Does it matter how the church worships?

II. God is seeking a certain type of worship – in spirit and truth (John 4:24).

    A. If worship can be "in spirit" then it can also be without spirit.

    B. If worship can be "in truth" then it can also be without truth.

III. Only those who worship in spirit and truth are true worshippers (John 4:23).

    A. If a person can be a true worshipper, a person can also be a false worshipper.

    B. Thus, there can be true worship and false worship.

IV. In this lesson we shall seek to understand the difference between true worship and false worship.

Discussion

I. Worshipping in Spirit

    A. Worship is induced by emotions of the human heart.

        1.) Such emotion should include love, thanksgiving, joy, and reverence.

        2.) These emotions are to be channeled properly – decently and orderly (1 Cor. 14:40).

        3.) There is a difference between worshipping with emotion and emotionalism.

    4.) Worship is not a reaction to the sentiments or feelings felt on the part of the worshipper.
  B. Worship is bowing before God (cf. Eph. 3:14).
  C. Worship is homage rendered to God.
    1.) To worship in spirit is to worship with the right emotions.
    2.) Worship in spirit occurs when the heart is in the right place.
    3.) True worship is offered to God according to His instructions.
II. What Does It Mean to Worship in Truth?
  A. What is truth?
    1.) God's word (John 17:17)
    2.) To worship in truth is to worship according to God's word.
  B. Which covenant?
    1.) Patriarchal, Jewish, or Christian?
    2.) The old covenant is nailed to the cross (Col. 2:14).
    3.) We have a new covenant in Christ (Heb. 8-9).
  C. Worship according to Christ's covenant includes:
    1.) The "Lord's Day," which is the first day of the week (Rev.1:10; Acts 20:7; 1 Cor. 16:1-2).
    2.) The church is to assemble on that day (Heb. 10:25; 1 Cor. 11:20).

3.) On that day we are to do the following acts of worship:

a.) Lord's Supper (Matt. 26:26-28; Acts 20:7; 1 Cor. 11:23-29)[1][2]

b.) Prayer to God in Christ's name (Luke 11:1-4; John 14:13)[3]

c.) Singing (Eph. 5:19-20; Col. 3:16-17)[4]

d.) Giving (1 Cor. 16:1-2; 2 Cor. 9:7ff)[5]

e.) Preaching (1 Cor. 14:34-35; 1 Pet. 4:11)[6]

---

[1] The Lord's Supper serves a commemorative purpose and significance. We do not do this in order to remember Him, but because we remember Him. C.R. Nichol and R.L. Whiteside, *Sound Doctrine*, vol. 1, (Nashville, TN: Gospel Advocate Company, 2001), 165.

[2] Various theories pertaining to the Lord's Supper are apparent. Some believe the Lord's Supper is a sacrament which bestows grace when partaken. Others believe the Lord's Supper is an ordinance of the church and that the church has authority to decide when it should be observed. It is also believed that the Lord's Supper should be a closed communion, meaning that only members of the church are allowed to partake. Some even believe that the Lord's Supper was never intended to be perpetually observed and, as a result, do not observe it in any form.

[3] Some controversy has occurred in recent years regarding prayers to Jesus. Acts 1:24-25 seems to be the most plausible passage to support the idea; however, it is unclear whether the apostles were addressing Christ or the Father from the text. We are certain that Jesus has instructed us to pray to the Father (Luke 11:1-4). The safer course is to do what is certainly right.

[4] Various arguments have been made to support the use of mechanical instruments in Christian worship. The following passages speak of the music of the early church: Rom. 15:9, 11; 1 Cor. 14:15, 26; Eph. 5:19; Col. 3:16; Heb. 2:12; James 5:13. No acceptance of mechanical instruments is found in the NT or for several centuries following the apostles.

[5] The Lord's Day contribution of the saints is distinct from the practice of Old Testament Jewish tithing. The Jews paid three tithes according to the law. Samuel later warned Israel that the king they desired would require a tenth to sustain his rule (1 Sam. 8: 15-17). They paid a priestly tithe (Lev. 27:30-33), a festival tithe (Deut. 14:22-27), and a tithe for the poor (Deut. 14:28-29).

III. Worship in Spirit and Truth[7]

Act	Spirit (Attitude)	Truth (Authority)
Lord's Supper	Examine self; Remembering Christ	Unleavened bread, fruit of vine, first day of week
Prayer	Thanksgiving; humility	To God through Christ
Singing	Grace in the heart	Singing, spiritual songs, everyone
Giving	Cheerfully with purpose	A collection, as prospered; first day of week
Preaching	In love, with meekness; receive with meekness	Speak truth; preach Christ not self

Conclusion

I. When we worship in spirit and truth, we enjoy one of the greatest and purest blessings of life.

II. God is seeking worship in spirit and in truth. If we truly love Him, let us worship Him as He has commanded.

---

[6] Women are prohibited from praying, preaching, or teaching in the church's assembly. These instructions (specifically in 1 Tim. 2) prepare the way for Paul's instructions concerning elders and deacons being husbands of one wife – denoting male leadership in the church (1 Tim. 3). Women have a function men do not have in child bearing (1 Tim. 2:15) and men have a function women do not have in leadership in the church.

[7] This chart is intended to illustrate each act of New Testament worship when conducted in the right spirit and with the instructions authorized in scripture.

The Work of the Church

Introduction

I. The work of the church can be classified under three headings: evangelism, edification, and benevolence.

II. We must do these works according to the authority of God.

   A. The Scriptures are profitable for every good work (2 Tim. 3:16-17).

   B. If the church will work according to God's plan, it will have more than enough to do the work He has commanded.

III. God's pattern not only points to the method in which these things are done, but also the manner.

   A. Worship is not the only thing to be conducted in spirit and truth.

   B. Everything we do for God should be done in spirit and truth.

Discussion

I. Evangelism (What and How?)

   A. The church is the only institution authorized to teach all nations (Matt. 28:18-20).

   B. Evangelism is teaching and preaching the word of God.

      1.) Evangelism can be public.

      2.) Evangelism can be private – "personal" evangelism.

3.) "I kept back nothing that was helpful, but proclaimed it to you, and taught you publicly and from house to house" (Acts 20:20).

4.) The church is unlimited in its scope for good.

C. Some relevant scriptures:

1.) "For since, in the wisdom of God, the world through wisdom did not know God, it pleased God through the foolishness of the message preached to save those who believe" (1 Cor. 1:21).

2.) "For I determined not to know anything among you except Jesus Christ and Him crucified" (1 Cor. 2:2).

3.) For we preach not ourselves, but Christ Jesus the Lord; and ourselves your servants for Jesus' sake" (2 Cor. 4:5).

4.) "Speaking the truth in love, may grow up in all things into Him who is the head – Christ" (Eph. 4:15).

5.) "Preach the word! Be ready in season and out of season. Convince, rebuke, exhort, with all longsuffering and teaching" (2 Tim. 4:2).

6.) "If anyone speaks, let him speak as the oracles of God. If anyone ministers, let him do it as with the ability which God supplies, that in all things God may be glorified through Jesus Christ, to whom belong the glory and the dominion forever and ever. Amen" (1 Pet. 4:11).

D. In summary, evangelism is the teaching and preaching of the word of God. The church is commanded to do it. It is unlimited in its scope of teaching.

II. Edification (What and How?)

A. Edification is the building up, or uplifting, spiritually of the body of Christ.

B. The work of the church includes building up one another in love (Eph. 4:11-16).

1.) We build up by Bible teaching (Eph. 4:11-12).

a.) Godly edifying is in faith (1 Tim. 1:4).

b.) Faith comes by Bible teaching (Rom. 10:17).

2.) We build up by every part working together (Eph. 4:16).

a.) Every joint is supplying something to build up the body; every part should be doing its share.

b.) The body of Christ has no non-essential members (1 Cor. 12:21-22).

3.) We build up by loving one another (Eph. 4:16).

a.) Love edifies (1 Cor. 8:1).

b.) Every part works together because of the love they share for the body.

C. A church that is not committed to edification is a church that is not committed to Christ.

1.) As we do to the church, we do to Christ (Matt. 25:40).
2.) As we do it not to the church, we do it not to Christ (Matt. 25:45).
3.) "For both He who sanctifies and those who are being sanctified are all of one, for which reason He is not ashamed to call them brethren" (Heb. 2:11).

D. To love Christ is to love His church.
1.) "If someone says, 'I love God,' and hates his brother, he is a liar; for he who does not love his brother whom he has seen, how can he love God whom he has not seen? And this commandment we have from Him: that he who loves God must love his brother also" (1 John 4:20-21).
2.) The things which are beloved of God must be important to those who seek to be beloved of God.

E. Edification is a work that requires work.
1.) We must think about how we might edify each other (Rom. 14:19; 2 Cor. 12:19; Heb. 10:24).
2.) We must act upon our considerations to bring spiritual growth and encouragement to the body of Christ.

F. Once again, the church is the only institution commanded to edify the church.
1.) If we do not edify ourselves, we will not be edified.

          2.) We cannot find edification in the world.

          3.) We need each other to build up one another.

III.   Benevolence (What and How?)

    A. The church is to be a charitable and benevolent group of people.

        1.) Once again, the church is the only institution ordained by God with the obligation to do good unto all men (Gal. 6:9-10).

          a.) Christians can be helped by the church (2 Cor. 8:12).

          b.) Non-Christians can be helped by the church (2 Cor. 8:13; Acts 24:17).

          c.) The church is authorized to help any person unable to help himself or herself.[1]

        2.) The local congregation is to fund her work through:

          a.) Lord's day collection (1 Cor. 16:1-2)

          b.) Help from sister congregations (Rom. 15:26)

          c.) Contributions taken as needed or necessary (Acts 4:37)[2]

    B. The church is completely sufficient to do what God would have us to do (2 Cor. 9:8).

---

[1] It is important to make this point in response to the doctrine of limited benevolence, which would have the church helping only other Christians financially from its treasury.

[2] It is important to make this point as the church is not authorized to sell goods or services to fund its work. Unfortunately, this is becoming a more common practice. Obviously, it is not charity if we charge for it.

      1.) The church is completely capable of doing the work God has given her if the church will only follow His instructions.

      2.) Churches can even decide to work together if the work requires more help.

          a.) Churches can send help directly to another congregation (Acts 11:27-30).

          b.) Churches might decide to work cooperatively with other congregations (Rom. 15:26).

  C. The church that has the right spirit will have the right works.

      1.) Be ready-minded (2 Cor. 8:11).

      2.) Be steadfast (1 Cor. 15:58).

      3.) Be not weary (Gal. 6:9).

      4.) Be not slothful (Heb. 6:10-12).

      5.) Be pure in your religion (James 1:27).

      6.) Be compassionate (Heb. 10:34).

      7.) Be like Christ (Luke 10:30-37).

      8.) Be faithful in what you have (2 Cor. 8:12).

      9.) Be faithful in what you do (Col. 3:17).

      10.) Give the glory to God (Acts 2:45-47).

Conclusion

I.   Let us determine to work in spirit and truth.

II.   When the church works in spirit and truth, God is glorified, the church is edified, and souls are sanctified.

The Falling Away

Introduction

I. The church at Thessalonica was being led to believe the Lord was soon to return (2 Thess. 2:2).

   A. Some in the first century were teaching that the resurrection had already occurred (2 Tim. 2:17-18).

   B. Others were teaching that the resurrection was not going to occur (1 Cor. 15:12).

   C. Paul is clear in his teaching on the return of Christ and the resurrection (1 Thess. 4:13 ff; 2 Thess. 1:7-10).

   D. He states in this passage (2 Thess. 2:1-12), that a falling away will occur before the Lord's return.

II. What does it mean to fall away (2 Thess. 2:3)?

   A. The "falling away" (KJV; NKJV) is translated "rebellion" (ESV) and "apostasy" (NASB).

      1.) Each of these translations is accurate.

      2.) We derive our English word *apostasy* from this Greek word *apostasia*.

         a.) *apostasia* – a defection from truth; rebellion; abandonment; to forsake[1]

         b.) *apostasia* is the feminine form of *apostasion*, which means literally to divorce or separate; to repudiate.

---

[1] This definition is compiled from various Greek lexicons.

- B. Therefore, the "falling away" of 2 Thessalonians 2:1-12 is a defection, rebellion, abandonment, forsaking, divorcing and repudiation from/of the truth of the gospel *en masse*.

III. The nature of the falling away:
- A. It was *gradual* in that in did not occur suddenly or at a specific point in time.
  - 1.) It was already at work during the time of Paul (v.7).
  - 2.) Yet, it had not reached its full effect (vv.2-3).
- B. It is *ever digressing* in new doctrines and traditions which continue to develop and take people farther away from God's New Testament church (2 Tim. 3:13).
  - 1.) Make no mistake, a falling away has occurred.
  - 2.) At any time and at any place a person attempts to oppose and exalt himself above God, he is the living embodiment of the man of sin.
  - 3.) I believe a figure of speech known as *personification* is being used in this passage.
  - 4.) Accordingly, the "man of sin" is representative of the agenda of rebellion on the part of those who do not believe the truth but have pleasure in unrighteousness (v.12).
  - 5.) It could apply to the coming heresy of Gnosticism or to the Judaizing teachers of the first century. Or,

it could apply to something to come to fruition centuries later.

6.) It could apply to any false teacher or religious leader who has sought to take people away from the truth. The man of lawless may be a movement, institution, system, or individual. Whatever the case, his doom is certain.[2]

Discussion

I. Falling Away from Biblical Leadership[3]

A. Paul's Warning and Prophecy (Acts 20:28-30):

1.) False teachers would arise from among the elders *speaking perverse things, to draw away disciples after them.*

2.) These were considered *grievous wolves* that would not *spare the flock.*

3.) While Paul was speaking specifically to the elders of the church at Ephesus, his warning applies to churches everywhere.

B. The second century saw the beginning of this great apostasy.

---

[2] Raymond C. Kelcy, *The Letters of Paul to the Thessalonians* (Abilene, TX: ACU Press, 1984), 164.

[3] For more information on the history of the great apostasy see: F.W. Mattox, *The Eternal Kingdom* (Delight, AR: Gospel Light Publishing Co., 1961); John F. Rowe, *History of Reformatory Movements* (Indianapolis, IN: Faith and Facts Press, 1993); J.W. Shepherd, *The Church, the Falling Away, and the Restoration* (Nashville, TN: Gospel Advocate Co., 1967).

1.) "Presiding elders" became common practice with such historic examples as Irenaeus of Lyons, Clement of Rome, Ignatius of Antioch, and Cyprian of Carthage (in the third century).
2.) The "presiding elder" sought to have the preeminence or be the "chief elder" among the eldership in which he was to serve.
   a.) Jerome argued that the practice of presiding elders was a necessary expedient to still strife in the church.
   b.) A New Testament example of this attitude is found in Diotrephes who loved having preeminence in the church so much that he would not receive the great and beloved apostle John (3 John 9-10).
   c.) Elders are to oversee the congregation as a group of men. The church is to obey "them" (Heb. 13:7, 17).
3.) The doctrine of "apostolic succession" began being taught in the second century.
   a.) Some felt because of the close relationship they or their congregation had with various apostles in times past that they had a greater role or prestige in the church than did others.

      b.) An historic example of this theory in practice was Clement of Rome's letter to the church at Corinth, *1 Clement*. He felt because he was the presiding bishop of Rome that he had succeeded the apostles Peter and Paul and, therefore, had the authority to admonish the quarreling church at Corinth. His counsel, however, was far different from that of any New Testament writer as he encouraged them to honor the elders at Corinth even though a kind of "super elder" had already emerged.

      c.) Paul was the last apostle (1 Cor. 15:8). Nowhere in scripture do we find the doctrine of apostolic succession.

C. The third century saw a priesthood begin to be patterned after the Old Testament pattern for the Jewish priesthood rather than after the New Testament pattern for the church.

  1.) Cyprian was instrumental in advancing this cause.

  2.) The office of "priest" began to be viewed as a mediating office just as the Levitical priesthood of the Jewish covenant.

  3.) Ordaining ceremonies began to be held for the purpose of consecrating a "propitiating priest."

4.) Jesus is our propitiation (Rom. 3:25; 1 John 2:2; 4:10), High Priest (Heb. 4:14 ff.), and Mediator (1 Tim. 2:5).

5.) Every Christian is considered a holy and royal priesthood collectively (1 Pet. 2:5, 9).

D. By the fourth century elderships began to take on the pattern of the Roman magistrates of the day.

1.) A Roman magistrate would be responsible to the emperor for the region of communities (diocese) under his control.

2.) Presiding bishops in the congregations were already common by this time.

3.) The next step was to make a "presiding bishop" over the presiding bishops in that area.

4.) Rome, Constantinople, Antioch, Alexandria, and Jerusalem were the five main dioceses in which each had a "chief elder" of the chief elders.

5.) Councils began to be held by these chief elders to determine doctrines for the church.

a.) The most historic being the Council of Nicea in 325.

b.) The traditions and doctrines decided in such councils were accepted as being just as authoritative as the scriptures by those who held them.

6.) Congregational autonomy was forfeited to these bishops and their councils.

E. The "Universal Bishop"

1.) Although various men had claimed this title it was not recognized until 606 when Boniface, the Bishop at Rome assumed the title.

2.) The "universal bishop" is known today as the "pope" or "holy father" – a title never found in the Bible!

II. The Falling Away from Biblical Teaching

A. Christ's Prophecy (Matt. 7:15-20)

B. Paul's Prophecy (1 Tim. 4:1-3; 2 Tim. 3:1-9, 13; 4:3-4)

C. Peter's Prophecy (2 Pet. 2:1-3)

D. Jude's prophecy (Jude 4-19)

E. Historic Examples:

1.) "Original Sin" – 2nd century

a.) Man is not born in sin, but in the light of Christ (John 1:9).

b.) Man is not born dead, but alive (Rom. 7:9).

2.) "Sprinkling and Pouring" – 251 AD (made equal to immersion at the Council of Ravenna in 1311)

a.) Baptism is an immersion (Rom. 6:3-4; Col. 2:12-13).

b.) *Baptidzo* – to dip, to plunge, to bury, to cover up

3.) "Purgatory" – 5th-6th century

      a.) The blood of Christ cleanses us from all sin (1 John 1:7, 9).

      b.) In Christ, God will remember our sins no more (Heb. 8:12; 10:17).

4.) "Mechanical Instruments of Music in Worship" – 660 AD (officially accepted in 1250)

      a.) Eight different times we read of the music of the church in the NT. Every time singing is the music we find.[4]

      b.) *A Capella* – the music of the church

5.) Martin Luther introduced the doctrine of salvation by faith alone in the 16th century.

      a.) Man is saved by faith, an obedient faith (Heb. 5:8-9).

      b.) The only time the phrase "faith alone" is found in the NT is James 2:24 – "not by faith alone."

6.) John Calvin reintroduced Augustine's teachings in the 16th century.

      a.) Original sin, predestination of the soul, limited atonement, unconditional election, etc.

      b.) Calvin's teachings can be answered by understanding the free will of man, the nature of

---

[4] Romans 15:9, 11; 1 Corinthians 14:15, 26; Ephesians 5:19; Colossians 3:16; Hebrews 2:12; James 5:13

choice and sin, the conditions of obedience in the gospel, and the possibility of apostasy.

7.) The doctrine of "papal infallibility" was not proclaimed until 1870.

a.) This doctrine asserts that the Pope is infallible in his decrees while ruling in an official capacity.

b.) Thus, his infallibility comes and goes!

c.) One needs only to study a history of the Pope to find that many of the most wicked tyrants and perverts ever to live have held this title.

F. If these things are of God, why can we not find them in the scriptures given by God for Christians to follow?

1.) If they were from God, we would find them in the word of God (2 Tim. 3:16-17).

2.) If they are not from God, they must be rejected as being another gospel (Gal. 1:6-9).

III. The Leadership and the Teaching of the Church Will Stand or Fall Together.

A. Leadership Affects Teaching

1.) If the leadership of a congregation is faithful, the teaching will be sound in doctrine.

2.) If the leadership is not faithful, the teaching will be unsound or at least incomplete in doctrine.

B. Teaching Affects Leadership

- 1.) If the teaching is sound over a prolonged period, the leadership that will be developed from such teaching will be faithful.
- 2.) If the teaching is unsound or incomplete over a prolonged period, the leadership that will be developed will be unfaithful.

C. We must be aware of the possibility of heresy entering the church through its leadership and teaching.
- 1.) The passage we have been studying warn of: "The coming of the *lawless one* is according to the working of Satan, with all power, signs, and lying wonders, and with all unrighteous deception among those who perish, because they did not receive the love of the truth, that they might be saved. And for this reason God will send them strong delusion, that they should believe the lie, that they all may be condemned who did not believe the truth but had pleasure in unrighteousness" (2 Thess. 2:10-12).
- 2.) "Beloved, do not believe every spirit, but test the spirits, whether they are of God; because many false prophets have gone out into the world" (1 John 4:1).

Conclusion

I. Can a falling away occur today?

    A. Anytime and at any place a church can fall away by failing to follow God's word in its leadership, doctrine, and practice.

    B. By so doing, churches have formed a pattern for apostasy rather than following God's pattern for the church.

II. What can we do to prevent a falling away?

    A. Only scripturally qualified men should serve as elders and deacons.

    B. Only sound doctrine should be taught with a zero tolerance for anything else.

III. Which pattern shall we follow?

    A. Shall we choose to follow God's pattern for the church and be the church of the New Testament?

    B. Or, shall we follow this pattern for apostasy and separate ourselves from the love of God.

The Sin of Denominationalism

Introduction

I. To understand denominationalism, one must know something about church history.

    A. Until Catholicism there was no denominationalism. Observe the steps toward division:

        1.) Roman Catholicism

        2.) The Great Schism of 1054 between East (Greek Orthodox) and West (Roman Catholic)

        3.) The Protestant Reformation Movement

    B. Denominationalism is the re-forming and re-naming (denominating) of other churches to distinguish them from (and in protest of) Catholicism and each other.

    C. The fallacy in this concept is the re-forming of man-made churches rather than the restoring of true New Testament Christianity.

II. The only thing denominationalism has accomplished is to divide those who would otherwise be following Jesus.[1]

    A. Because of the influence of denominationalism, people sincerely believe all churches are denominations and all denominations make up the one church.

---

[1] For a survey of the unscriptural doctrines and practices of mainline denominations and cults see Jerry Moffitt, *Denominational Doctrines* (Damon, TX: Firm Foundation Publishing House, 1996).

1.) For those in denominations, it is no doubt easier to accept this view than to accept the biblical teaching of one church made up only of those who have obeyed the one gospel.

2.) Because of the belief that all churches are denominations, those in denominationalism believe no denomination has a right to judge or condemn another denomination.[2]

3.) If this were true, they would be correct; no denomination (man-made church) is better than another denomination (man-made church).

4.) However, no denomination can rival the Lord's church; the one church of the Bible.

Discussion

I. Denominationalism Opposes Biblical Unity[3]

A. Christ prayed and died for the unity of His followers (John 17:17; Eph. 2:13-17).

B. Paul condemned the division at Corinth (1 Cor. 1:10-13).

C. If any man should promote any doctrine different than Paul's inspired teaching, he should be accursed (Gal. 1:6-9).

---

[2] For further discussion of this objection see: Thomas B. Warren, *The Bible Only Makes Christians Only* (Henderson, TN: Hester Publications, 2005), 183–193.

[3] A book which must be considered on this topic is James D. Bales, *Soils and Seeds of Sectarianism* (Kansas City, MO: Old Paths Book Club, 1947).

    D. Anyone unwilling to walk by the same rule, and mind the same thing, as did the apostle Paul is an enemy of the cross of Christ (Phil. 3:16-19).

II. Denominationalism Opposes Biblical Church Offices[4]

    A. We read of a plurality of elders or pastors in every church (Acts 14:23).

    B. Denominationalism promotes a single elder or pastoral system.

        1.) Each church must be self-governing (Acts 20:28).

        2.) We do not read of any association established to oversee congregations in an area.

    B. We read of deacons being the husband of one wife (1 Tim. 3:12).

    C. We read of the office of preacher being filled by faithful men (2 Tim. 2:2).

        1.) Women are admonished to "learn in silence with all subjection" (1 Tim. 2:11).

        2.) Paul forbids them "to teach, nor to usurp authority over the man, but to be in silence" (v.12).

        3.) God's commandment pertains specifically to the assembly of the saints and the public proclamation of the gospel (cf. 1 Cor. 14:34-35).

III. Denominationalism Opposes Christ's Preeminence

---

[4] See: Stafford North, *Handbook on Church Doctrines* (Edmond, OK: Landmark Books, 1999), 87–107.

- A. Christ is to have the preeminence in the church in all things (Col. 1:18).
- B. Does Christ have the preeminence if we call ourselves something other than Christians (Acts 11:26; Isa. 42:8; 62:2; 65:15)?
- C. Does Christ have the preeminence if we follow the teachings of men rather than the word of God?

IV. Denominationalism Opposes Christ's Authority
- A. Whatever we do in word or deed must be done in the name of the Lord (Col. 3:17).
    - 1.) To do something in His name is to do it with His authority and approval.
    - 2.) Christ has all authority over His church (Eph. 1:22-23).
- B. Man will be judged by the word of Christ (John 12:48).
- C. If Christ has all authority and we will be judged by His word, what authority does man's opinion hold?
- D. Rather than seek Bible authority for their practices, denominations give feelings and wrongful interpretations of the Scriptures the authority.

V. Denominationalism Opposes True Worship
- A. God is seeking true worship (John 4:21-24).
- B. God's word is truth (John 17:17).
    - 1.) Truth and fulfillment are found in Christ (John 1:17; Matt. 5:17).

  2.) To worship in truth is to worship according to the covenant of Christ rather than God's covenant with the Jews (Heb. 8:6-7).

 C. Man is not at liberty to choose how he will worship God.

  1.) God has given us commands for worship.

  2.) When man worships according to his will rather than God's, it is "will worship" (Col. 2:20-23).

VI. Denominationalism Opposes the Biblical Doctrine of Man's Salvation

 A. We do not find one line of scripture which teaches a sinner's prayer, mourner's bench, or the oft-claimed "outward sign of an inward grace."

 B. Neither do we find a passage which teaches the unconditional "Once Saved Always Saved" doctrine.

 C. Why obey a teaching not taught in the Bible when you can read and obey these commands from your Bible?

  1.) Believe (John 8:24)

  2.) Repent (Luke 13:3, 5)

  3.) Confess Christ (Rom. 10:9-10)

  4.) Be Baptized (Mark 16:16) and become born again into His kingdom (John 3:3-5).

Conclusion

I. Man has an alternative to denominationalism.

 A. He can be a Christian and only a Christian.

        B. He can obey the gospel and the Lord will add him to His church (Acts 2:47).
II.   Not every church is a denomination.
        A. One church was established before any denomination existed (Matt. 16:18).
        B. One church will endure long after all denominations are consumed (Heb. 12:25-29).

Is One Church as Good as Another?

Introduction

I. It is easier for a person in a denomination to believe one church is as good as another rather than to believe there is only one church.

　A. After all, if all churches are denominations, how arrogant would it be to believe your denomination is better than my denomination!

　B. If the denominational world is right, and all churches are denominations and all denominations make up the church, such studies as this should cease and disappear forevermore from the face of the earth.

II. It is easier for some to believe one church is as good as another to keep from accepting the destiny of many loved ones.

　A. Some would rather disregard what God has said on the subject than condemn a loved one.

　B. Consider, please, if this is true and a loved one of yours or mine stands condemned, what reason does that give for us to reject the truth?

　　1.) Each soul will give an account of their own life to God (Rom. 14:12).

　　2.) Why should we think that our rejection of truth would in some way change God's judgment upon another who likewise rebelled?

       3.) A loved one's refusal to believe the Bible on this or any other subject in no way forces you or me to make the same mistake.

       4.) Man has no authority to rebel against God on this or any other point.

Discussion

I. The Lord's Church (Matt. 16:13-19)[1]

   A. If one church is as good as another church, why didn't the Lord build many churches?

   B. If one church is as good as another church, is this other church as good as the church the Lord said was His church?

   C. Can another church be as good as the church built by Jesus?

       1.) If so, who is this builder as good as Jesus?

       2.) Where do we read of this builder in the Scriptures?

       3.) By what authority did he build?

II. The Lord's House (1 Tim. 3:15)

   A. Is one family as good as God's family?

   B. Is one father as good as our Heavenly Father?

   C. What would another church uphold if the truth is already upheld by the Lord's church?

---

[1] For similar argumentation see: F. B. Srygley, *The New Testament Church* (Nashville, TN: Gospel Advocate Co., 2001); Thomas W. Phillips, *The Church of Christ* (Cincinnati, OH: Standard Publishing Co., 1909).

D. If the church established in the New Testament upholds the truth, can there be any other "Bible-believing" church?

E. Can another house be as good as the Lord's house?

1.) If so, who is the head of this house which is claimed to be as good as God's house?

2.) Upon what foundation does this other house sit since only the church is founded upon hearing and doing the word of God? (Matt. 7:23 ff.)

3.) If hearing and doing the word of God will bring you into His house, whose word must you hear and do to be brought into another house?

III. The Lord's Body (Eph. 4:4-6)

A. How many bodies are said to exist?

B. What is this body?

1.) Read Eph. 1:22-23.

2.) In this one body we are reconciled to God by the cross (Eph. 2:16).

C. Seeing that there is only one *body*, there can only be one *church*.

D. If we are reconciled in the one *body*, we are reconciled in the one *church*.

E. If one church is as good as another church:

1.) Why is there only one church mentioned in the Bible?

        2.) Who has the preeminence in another church since Christ already has the preeminence in His church?

        3.) Is there reconciliation in another church?

        4.) If so, how? For there is only *one* body reconciled by the cross.

    F. Can another body be as good as the Lord's body?

        1.) If so, who is as good as the Lord?

        2.) Who died to establish another body?

        3.) Was his death as good as the Lord's death?

IV. The Lord's Blood (Acts 20:28)

    A. If one church is as good as another, why did Christ shed His blood for only one church?

        1.) Whose blood purchased another church if Christ's blood purchased only His church?

        2.) If there is another church, is there another means of atonement?

        3.) If there is another means of atonement, why did Christ have to die for our sins?

    B. If one church is as good as another, then whose blood is as good as Christ's blood?

V. The Lord's Authority (Acts 2:41, 47)

    A. If one church is as good as another church, who has authority to equal the Lord?

    B. Who will add you to another church if the Lord only adds to His church?

C. By what authority are you added or joined to another church?
   D. If all the saved are added to the Lord's church, are the lost in other churches?
   E. The Lord decides who He will and will not add to His church.
      1.) His decision is based upon our hearing and obeying His word.
      2.) When man gladly receives the word of God and obeys Him, the Lord adds that person to His church.

Conclusion

I. Man must do more than "join a Bible-believing church."
II. Man must be added by God to His church through obedience to the gospel.
   A. The Lord shed His blood to buy the church (Acts 20:28).
   B. The church belongs to and was built by the Lord (Matt. 16:18).
   C. The Lord's gospel calls the sinner out of the world (2 Thess. 2:14).
   D. The Lord adds us to His church (Acts 2:47).
   E. Truly no church can be a Bible-believing church without accepting the truth that the Lord has only one church.

III. Why belong to just any church when you can be a member of the Lord's church?
   A. Does it exist today?
      1.) Look for the pattern in scripture.
      2.) Does a church exist according to the pattern?
   B. Can man be added to it today?
      1.) Look for the plan of salvation in scripture.
      2.) Does a church exist which teaches the gospel plan of salvation?
   C. Can man reject it today? Will you reject it?

Why I Am a Member of the Church of Christ[1]

Introduction

I. Have you ever asked a person why he or she is of a certain religion?

    A. Answers usually vary – parents; spouse; friends; close to home.

    B. Seldom will someone say, "Because the Bible teaches me to be."

II. What if someone asked me why I am a member of the church of Christ?

    A. How should I answer (1 Pet. 3:15)?

    B. Such a question certainly is not a "foolish question" (2 Tim. 2:23-26).

Discussion

I. The Study of Scripture

    A. The Bible teaches us when the church began (Isa. 2; Dan. 2; Joel 2; Acts 2 or Mark. 9:1; Acts 1:8; Acts 2:4).

    B. The Bible teaches us how to become a member of this church (Acts 2:38-41, 47; Col. 1:13).

    C. The Bible teaches us of no other church (Eph. 1:22-23; 4:4-5; 1 Cor. 12:13).

II. The Study of Church History

---

[1] A necessary book to study by this title is Leroy Brownlow, *Why I am a Member of the Church of Christ* (Fort Worth, TX: Brownlow Publishing Co., 1973).

A. Denominate – to name again; two things needed with each denomination – a new name and a new creed.
B. Denominationalism began with a great falling way and continues down to this day (2 Thess. 2).
  1.) 3rd Century – Presiding Elders
  2.) 4th Century – Church Councils
  3.) 606 – Universal Bishop (break between East and West)
  4.) Denominations emerged to re-form Catholicism (Luther, Calvin, Church of England).
  5.) Then, denominations emerged in order to reform denominations (Knox, Wesley, and Smyth).
    a.) With each new denomination came a new name (sometimes names were given according to the doctrines which distinguished the group; sometimes names were given for their leaders).
    b.) With each new denomination came a new creed to set the group apart from others.
    c.) Within these creeds, we find a different beginning for that particular church; we find a different plan of salvation; we find a different organization; and we find different worship practices.
III. The Desire to be Saved
  A. One religious system originated with God and one religious system originated with man.

        a.) New Testament Christianity is a religious system.

        b.) Denominationalism is a religious system.

        c.) But they are not the same religious system.

    B. Restoration – men began to see this for themselves; fire in dry stubble; courage, perseverance, faith

    C. One must obey the Bible to be saved (Heb. 5:8-9; John 12:48; 2 Thess. 1:7-9; 1 Pet. 1:22-25; James 1:21; Mark 16:15-16).

    D. Obeying the doctrines and commandments of men will cause one to be lost (Matt. 15:1-9; Mark 7:6-13; Col. 2:8).

IV. The Desire to Save Others

    A. One must obey the Bible if he is going to help others to be saved (1 Tim. 4:16; Phil. 4:9).

    B. Otherwise he is just another case of the blind leading the blind (Matt. 15:14; Matt. 23).

Conclusion

I. Why am I am member of the church of Christ? The study of scripture; church history; the desire to be saved and to save others.

II. Why are you a member of the church to which you belong?

The Restoration Plea[1]

Introduction

I. We have been blessed to live in a country which grants its citizens the right to religious freedom unprecedented in this world's history.

II. More than two hundred years ago devout Bible students, preachers, and church leaders used this freedom to return to the teachings of the Bible and restore the church of the New Testament.[2]

    A. What is meant by *restoration*?

    B. To *restore* is to bring something back to its original state.

    C. To accomplish restoration, we seek to return to the Bible as a sole guide for matters of faith and practice.

    D. Our plea:

        1.) That professing Christians speak and practice the same thing

        2.) That all who desire to follow Christ share all things in common pertaining to faith in Him

---

[1] For further study see James D. Bales, *Restoration, Reformation, or Revelation* (Shreveport, LA: Lambert Book House, 1975).

[2] For a concise overview of the restoration movement in America see V. Glenn McCoy, *Return to the Old Paths: A History of the Restoration Movement* (Yorba Linda, CA: McCoy Publications, 1998); Andrew D. Erwin, *Select Studies in Restoration History: 1700-Present Day* (Charleston, AR: Cobb Publishing, 2017).

3.) That the only way this can be accomplished is by each person's return to the Bible, and the Bible alone, for a guide to all things religious

4.) To lay aside all practices, names, offices, titles, traditions, creeds, councils, Catholicism, and denominationalism which remain unauthorized by commands, examples, or necessary and proper inferences from the text

5.) To lay aside all such things which are restricted by the silence of the Scriptures, created by man, thus hindering a union of believers and one's acceptable service to God

III. In seeking to restore biblical Christianity, pious souls have used four maxims to guide them. I would like to share these maxims with you as a basis for our lesson.

Discussion

I. "No creed but the Bible"

   A. A Biblical Maxim

      1.) 2 Tim. 3:16-17; 2 Pet. 1:3

      2.) John 12:48

   B. How can we obey this biblical truth?

      1.) Respect for the Bible and its authority is the key.

      2.) Place the Bible in its rightful place and keep it there. "Buy the truth and sell it not."

II. "Speak where the Bible speaks and be silent where the Bible is silent."
   A. A Biblical Maxim:
      1.) It was true of the Old Law (Deut. 4:2).
      2.) It is true of the Law of Christ (Rev. 22:18-19).
   B. How can we obey this biblical truth?
      1.) Do not think of men above that which is written (1 Cor. 4:6).
      2.) Do not compare yourself with others (2 Cor. 10:12).
      3.) The word of God must be our standard – nothing more, nothing less (John 12:48; Phil. 3:16).
III. "Do Bible things in Bible ways and call Bible things by Bible names."
   A. A Biblical Maxim:
      1.) In the Old Testament, the tabernacle had to be made according to the pattern (Exo. 26:30).
      2.) In the New Testament, we have a pattern to follow.[3]
         a.) A pattern of obedience (1 Tim. 1:16).
         b.) A pattern for good works (Titus 2:7).
   B. How can we obey this biblical truth?
      1.) Determine to live by faith (Rom. 10:17).
      2.) Defeat the attitude that would have us do otherwise – vanity (2 Cor. 10:18).

---

[3] For further study about the pattern for matters of faith practice see Goebel Music, *Behold the Pattern* (Colleyville, TX: Goebel Music Publications, 1991).

IV. "In matters of faith – unity; in matters of opinion – liberty; in all things – charity."
   A. A Biblical Maxim:
      1.) Unity in matters of faith (1 Cor. 1:10-13).
      2.) Liberty in matters of opinion; live in peace (2 Cor. 13:11).
      3.) Charity (love) in all things (1 Cor. 13:4-7; 1 John 4:10-21)
   B. How can we obey this biblical truth?
      1.) By having Christ as the head of the body.
      2.) By realizing the member is not bigger than the body.

Conclusion

I. Some have asked if the restoration plea is valid today.
II. This author believes we can answer that question by asking two questions:
   A. If we practice these maxims in our approach to the Scriptures, will we be faithful to God?
   B. If we ignore these maxims in our approach to the Scriptures, will we inevitably return to the religious error from which our forefathers broke free?
   C. Any plea that biblically seeks to bring men closer to God and ultimately home to heaven is a valid plea.
III. Will you be a restorer?
   A. The harvest remains white and the laborers few.

B. Will you help us and work with us to gain the lost and dying for Christ?

C. May all Christians everywhere devote themselves to this great cause, the cause of our Lord, the plea to be united in Him, the cause for which He prayed and died.

"Now the God of peace, that brought again from the dead our Lord Jesus, that great Shepherd of the sheep, through the blood of the everlasting covenant, Make you perfect in every good work to do his will, working in you that which is well pleasing in his sight, through Jesus Christ; to whom be glory for ever and ever. Amen."
(Hebrews 13:20-21)

Bibliography

Bales, James D. *Restoration, Reformation, or Revelation*. Shreveport, LA: Lambert Book House, 1975.

Bales, James D. *Soils and Seeds of Sectarianism*. Kansas City, MO: Old Paths Book Club, 1947.

Boll, R. H. *The Kingdom of God*. Louisville, KY: Word and Work, n.d.

Brents, T. W. *The Gospel Plan of Salvation*. Bowling Green, KY: Guardian of Truth Foundation, 1987.

Brownlow, Leroy. *Why I am a Member of the Church of Christ*. Fort Worth, TX: Brownlow Publishing Company, 1973.

Erwin, Andrew D. *Select Studies in Restoration History: 1700-Present Day*. Charleston, AR: Cobb Publishing, 2017.

Ferguson, Everett. *The New Testament Church*, 3rd ed. Abilene, TX: ACU Press, 2008.

Kelcy, Raymond C. *The Letters of Paul to the Thessalonians*. Abilene, TX: ACU Press, 1984.

Mattox, F. W. *The Eternal Kingdom*. Delight, AR: Gospel Light Publishing Co., 1961.

McCoy, V. Glenn. *Return to the Old Paths: A History of the Restoration Movement*. Yorba Linda, CA: McCoy Publications, 1998.

Moffitt, Jerry. *Denominational Doctrines*. Damon, TX: Firm Foundation Publishing House, 1996.

Mosheim, John Lawrence. *Ecclesiastical History*, vol.1. Rosemead, CA: Old Paths Book Club, 1959.

Music, Goebel. *Behold the Pattern*. Colleyville, TX: Goebel Music Publications, 1991.

Nichol, C. R. and R. L. Whiteside. *Sound Doctrine*, vol. 1. Nashville, TN: Gospel Advocate Company, 2001.

North, Stafford. *Handbook on Church Doctrines*. Edmond, OK: Landmark Books, 1999.

Phillips, Thomas W. *The Church of Christ*. Cincinnati, OH: Standard Publishing Company, 1909.

Rowe, John F. *History of Reformatory Movements*. Indianapolis, IN: Faith and Facts Publishing Company, 1993.

Shepherd, J. W. *The Church, the Falling Away, and the Restoration*. Nashville, TN: Gospel Advocate Company, 1967.

Srygley, F. B. *The New Testament Church*. Nashville, TN: Gospel Advocate Company, 2001.

Thayer, Joseph H. *Thayer's Greek English Lexicon of the New Testament*. Peabody, MA: Hendrickson Publishers, 2002.

Warren, Thomas, B. *The Bible Only Makes Christians Only*. Henderson, TN: Hester Publications, 2005.

Related Literature

Resources found to be valuable in the research and writing on this book but not listed in the footnotes and bibliography have been listed below.

Allen, F.G. *The Old Path Pulpit*. Nashville, TN: Gospel Advocate Company, 1940.

Bailey, George W. *Great Preachers of Today: Sermons of George W. Bailey*. Abilene, TX: Biblical Research Press, 1961.

Bales, James, D. *Messiah's Mission Accomplished*. Charleston, AR: Cobb Publishing, 2017.

Baxter, Batsell Barrett. *Family of God: A Study of the New Testament Church*. Nashville, TN: Gospel Advocate Company, 1980.

Boles, H. Leo and R.H. Boll. *Unfulfilled Prophecy: A Discussion on Prophetic Themes*. Nashville, TN: Gospel Advocate Company, 1954.

Borden, E.M., and Ben M. Bogard. *Borden-Bogard Debate*. Henderson, TN: Hester Publications, n.d.

Borden, E.M. *God's Eternal Purpose*. Oklahoma, City, OK: Herald of Truth Association, n.d.

Boswell, Ira M., and N.B. *Hardeman. Boswell-Hardeman Discussion on Instrumental Music in the Worship*. Bowling Green, KY: Guardian of Truth Foundation, n.d.

Brewer, G.C. *Brewer's Sermons*. Nashville, TN: Gospel Advocate Company, 1959.

Brewer, G.C. *Contending for the Faith*. Nashville, TN: Gospel Advocate Company, 1941.

Brewer, G.C. *The Model Church*. Nashville, TN: Gospel Advocate Company, 1957.

Brownlow, Leroy. *Seed for the Sower*. Fort Worth, TX: Brownlow Publishing Co., 1948.

Cloer, Eddie. *What Is the Church? Identifying the Nature and Design of the New Testament Church*. Searcy, AR: Resource Publications, 1993.

Cloer, Eddie. *God's Design for "The Church" Clarifying the Nature and Intention of the New Testament Church*. Searcy, AR: Resource Publications, 1993.

Coffman, E.C. *Complete Scripture Outlines*. Houston, TX: Herbert L. Coffman, 1958.

Cogdill, Roy E. *The New Testament Church*. Lufkin, TX: Gospel Guardian Company, 1959.

Crawford, C.C. *Sermon Outlines on the Restoration Plea*. Murfreesboro, TN: DeHoff Publications, 1956.

Dennis, Fred E. *Fifty Short Sermons*, vol. 1. Grand Rapids, MI: Eerdmans Publishing Company, 1942.

Dennis, Fred E. *Fifty Short Sermons*, vol. 2. Grand Rapids, MI: Eerdmans Publishing Company, 1944.

Ferguson, Everett. *The Church of Christ: A Biblical Ecclesiology for Today*. Grand Rapids, MI: Eerdmans Publishing Company, 1996.

Ferguson, Everett. The Everlasting Kingdom: The Kingdom of God in Scripture and in Our Lives. Abilene, TX: ACU Press, 1989.

Franklin, Benjamin. *The Gospel Preacher*, vol. 1. Delight, AR: Gospel Light Publishing Company, n.d.

Franklin, Benjamin. *The Gospel Preacher*, vol. 2. Delight, AR: Gospel Light Publishing Company, n.d.

Freed, A.G. *Sermons, Chapel Talks, and Debates*. Nashville, TN: Gospel Advocate Company, 1959.

Gardner, E. Claude (editor). *L.L. Brigance's Sermon Outlines*. Murfreesboro, TN: DeHoff Publications, 1951.

Gardner, E. Claude. *The Exceptional Church*. Henderson, TN: Hester Publications, 2016.

Hailey, Homer. *God's Eternal Purpose and the Covenants*. Louisville, KY: Religious Supply Incorporated, 1998.

Hardeman, N.B., and Ben M. Bogard. Hardeman-Bogard Debate. Nashville, TN: Gospel Advocate Company, 1938.

Hardeman, N.B. *Hardeman's Tabernacle Sermons*, vol. 2. Henderson, TN: Freed-Hardeman University, 1991.

Hardeman, N.B. *Hardeman's Tabernacle Sermons*, vol. 3. Henderson, TN: Freed-Hardeman University, 1990.

Hardeman, N.B. *Hardeman's Tabernacle Sermons*, vol. 4. Nashville, TN: Gospel Advocate Company, 1975.

Highers, Alan E., and W. Eural Bingham. *The Highers-Bingham Debate*. Corinth, MS: Pervie Nichols Publications, 1969.

Highers, Alan E., and Given O. Blakely. *The Highers-Blakely Debate on Instrumental Music in Worship*. Denton, TX: Valid Publications, 1988.

Lewis, John T. *The Voice of the Pioneers on Instrumental Music and Societies*. Nashville, TN: Gospel Advocate Company, 1932.

Malphurs, J.G. *The Glow from Golden Texts*. Dallas, TX: Christian Publishing Company, 1960.

Mauro, Philip. *The Gospel of the Kingdom with an Examination of Modern Dispensationalism.* Sterling, VA: Grace Abounding Ministries Incorporated, 1988.

McCord, Hugo. *Fifty Years of Lectures.* Atwood, TN: Atwood Church of Christ, Atwood, TN, n.d.

Miller, Max R. *Book, Chapter, and Verse Sermons.* Fayetteville, TN: Gospel Gleaner Publications, 2016.

Nichol, C. R., and R. L. Whiteside. *Sound Doctrine*, vol. 3. Nashville, TN: Gospel Advocate Company, 2001.

Nichol, C. R., and R. L. Whiteside. *Sound Doctrine*, vol. 4. Nashville, TN: Gospel Advocate Company, 2001.

Nichol, C. R., and A.S. Bradley. *The Nichol-Bradley Debate.* Clifton, TX: Nichol Publishing Company, 1907.

Nichol, C. R., and Charles R. Hensler. *Nichol-Hensler Debate.* Clifton, TX: Nichol Publishing Company, 1954.

Nichols, Gus. *Gus Nichols' Sermon Outlines.* Fort Worth, TX: Nichols Brothers Publishing Company, 1961.

Olbricht, Owen D. *The Kingdom of the Messiah.* Delight, AR: Gospel Light Publishing Company, 2019.

Pharr, David, R. *The Kingdom Come: The Truth about the Rapture.* Huntsville, AL: Publishing Designs Incorporated, 2003.

Porter, W. Curtis and Ben M. Bogard. *Porter-Bogard Debate.* Bowling Green, KY: Guardian of Truth Foundation, 2004.

Porter, W. Curtis and B. Sunday Myers. *Porter-Myers Debate.* Monette, AR: Porter's Book Shop, 1956.

Rowe, F.L. (editor). Pioneer Sermons and Addresses. Cincinnati, OH: F.L. Rowe, 1925.

Shepherd, J.W. (editor). *What is the New Testament Church? A Discussion between F.D. Syrgley and J.N. Hall.* Henderson, TN: Hester Publications, n.d.

Stroop, J. Ridley. *Restoration Ideas on Church Organization.* Nashville, TN: J. Ridley Stroop, n.d.

Stroop, J. Ridley. *The Church of the Bible*. Nashville, TN: J. Ridley Stroop, 1962.

Sweeney, John S. *Sweeney's Sermons*. Nashville, TN: Gospel Advocate Company, 1897.

Sweeney, Z.T. (editor). *New Testament Christianity*, vol. 1. Columbus, IN: Z.T. Sweeney, 1923.

Turner, Rex A. *Systematic Theology: Another Book on the Fundamentals of the Faith*. Montgomery, AL: Alabama Christian School of Religion, 1989.

Waggoner, Robert L. *Great Doctrines of the Bible*. Delight, AR: Gospel Light Publications, 2018.

Wallace, Jr., Foy E. *Number One Gospel Sermons*. Nashville, TN: Foy E. Wallace, Jr. Publications, 1967.

Wallace, Jr., Foy E. *The Gospel for Today*. Nashville, TN: Foy E. Wallace, Jr. Publications, 1967.

Wallace, G.K. *Autobiography and Retirement Sermons*. High Springs FL: Mary Lois Forrester, n.d.

Wallace, G.K. *Lectures on Denominational Dogmas*. Nashville, TN: Gospel Advocate Company, 1956.

Wharton, Edward C. *The Church of Christ: The Distinctive Nature of the New Testament Church*. Nashville, TN: Gospel Advocate Company, 1997.

Wilhite, J. Porter. *Modern Churches and the Church*. Shreveport, LA: Lambert Book House, 1956.

Winkler, Wendell. *The Church Everybody is Asking About*. Tuscaloosa, AL: Winkler Publications, 1988.

Wise, Melvin J. *The All-Sufficiency of the Gospel*. Shreveport, LA: Lambert Book House, 1964.

Woods, Guy N., and Roy E. Cogdill. *Woods-Cogdill Debate*. Nashville, TN: Gospel Advocate Company, 1958.

Made in the USA
Middletown, DE
07 September 2021